The Soul Connection

The Soul Connection

HOW TO ACCESS YOUR

HIGHER POWERS AND

DISCOVER YOUR TRUE SELF

Anne Jones

PIATKUS

First published in Great Britain in 2008 by Piatkus Books

Copyright © 2008 by Anne Jones

The moral right of the author has been asserted

A CIP catalogue record for this book
is available from the British Library

ISBN 978-0-7499-0967-3

Typeset in Bembo by Palimpsest Book Production, Grangemouth, Stirlingshire
Printed and bound in Great Britain by CPI William Clowes, Beccles NR34 7TL

Papers used by Piatkus Books are natural, renewable and recyclable
products made from wood grown in sustainable forests and certified
in accordance with the rules of the Forest Stewardship Council

Mixed Sources
Product group from well-managed
forests and other controlled sources
www.fsc.org Cert no. SGS-COC-004081
© 1996 Forest Stewardship Council
FSC

Piatkus Books
An imprint of
Little, Brown Book Group
100 Victoria Embankment
London EC4Y 0DY

An Hachette Livre UK Company
www.hachettelivre.co.uk

www.piatkus.co.uk

CONTENTS

Dedicated to Pops, the best father anyone ever had.

ACKNOWLEDGEMENTS

To Brenda for managing me and my life so that I have time for everything, Tessie for great food and for being my angel in the kitchen and home, Tony for being my rock and Mousie for her constant and unremitting stream of love, thank you so much and bless you.

Love and thanks to Cary for taking our vision for Africa and turning it into a reality, creating a focus for love and the abundance of my work.

Thank you to all the people who have asked for my help and have given me the opportunity to understand and develop my sense of the divine, both in them and in myself.

Thank you to John for the most amazing wisdom and advice.

Thank you to Helen and Gill and the Piatkus team for their support and belief, and for their great skills in taking my ham-fisted efforts and streamlining them into a sensible read!

INTRODUCTION

The Power of Reconnecting

*Let your ultimate goal be to allow spirit and divine energy
be your energy source and inspiration.*

Your life is a journey on which you travel in order to reach
a 'Nirvana' of inner peace, an inner knowing of self, and to
attain a permanent state of happiness. It can be likened to
climbing up a mountain – reaching up for a higher and
higher state of consciousness. In my book *The Ripple Effect*
I described a way in which you can create your own personal
guide book – your own path up the mountain – unrestricted
by rules and regulations created by others, following spiritual guidelines that suit you and that have been proven to
alleviate the stress of earthly living.

In *Opening Your Heart* I take you on a different aspect of
the journey, describing an inner path to open your heart to
give and receive love, to release and heal the pain and suffering
of your emotional and spiritual heart, which is the doorway
to receiving the love that nurtures every aspect of self:

physical, emotional, mental and spiritual. Through opening your heart you allow love to revitalise and heal your body and soul.

In this book I take you further on your personal spiritual journey, helping to reconnect you to your divine self and through this connection to integrate the divine powers that are your true essence. These powers open the way to an unimaginable source of inner strength and peace, and to the ability to create and attract the very best aspects of life, taking you on to your goal of joy and happiness.

Your greatest gift is to reconnect your soul with its divine partner - your Higher Self.

Three years ago I went to southern India with two friends and had an experience that changed my life. It triggered a major change in how I feel about myself and how I feel inside. It cleared away a sense of anxiety that I had felt all my life and it enhanced my intuitive and psychic powers. Since that time I have been able to access and channel amazing spiritual healing energies far beyond those I used before. Although I have given a full account of this experience in my book *Opening Your Heart*, here is a short résumé of what happened on and after that trip.

My visit took me to Pondicherry in south-west India, where I was drawn to visit one of the Catholic churches in the town. I sat and closed my eyes and was immediately visited by angels in a vision. The angels took me on an inner journey through my heart, showing me that it was not fully open to receive love. They explained that I had allowed old guilt and pain to create low self-esteem and feelings of un-worthiness that acted as barriers, preventing me from accepting love in its fullest aspect. Having shown me the four different chambers of the spiritual heart and how these affect the love we give and receive in our lives, they introduced me to the divine spark within that is the core energy of everyone, often referred to as the God within us. They then proceeded to guide me to ways in which I could open and heal my heart.

A week after my return from India I gathered with the friends who had travelled with me for a 'gratitude cere-mony', a thank you to everyone who had helped us on our holiday and had affected us in some way. After we had enjoyed recalling all the amazing things that had happened we sat quietly and relaxed. Suddenly I felt myself being lifted – it felt as if my whole body was rising, although it was in fact just my spirit that rose high above my head. I felt a sense of great peace and a lightness, as though all my cares were taken away. I then experienced a sense of exaltation, a feeling of wonderment and of 'coming home'.

After a while the wonder of the moment subsided, but since then I have never entirely lost that sense of connec-tion. I realised soon afterwards that I had in that moment made a full connection to my Higher Self – my Divine Presence or I AM as it's sometimes called. Subsequently I have worked on clearing the way, on releasing all the barriers that prevented this connection from becoming complete.

I have never felt better in my life since I reclaimed my own divine self, not only acknowledging it but integrating that part of me from which I had been separated a long, long time ago. I can now create my own life – manifesting simply and effortlessly. I feel good inside and, even if I am challenged by the upsets that everyday life throws up, it takes only a little time for me to re-establish a calm disposition. My healing work has grown more effective, for I am now working with spirit, not on my own, and I can now tap into the immense power of the universal consciousness. I am on my way to a complete accordance and connection to God, and this brings a sense of completeness and connection to everything and everyone else.

When my heart opened I thought that I had it all, but there was more! Since then I have progressed further, recognising and acknowledging that I am created from divine energies of love. Now everything I do is easy and effortless, whether it be writing, giving talks or healing sessions, or just managing my life from day to day. I feel fearless and less easily overawed by life and its challenges – I feel strong and full of purpose. And, on a lighter note, I feel and am told that I even look younger – now there's an incentive for you!

The changes this connection has brought to me and the powers that I can now claim have motivated me to help others to get connected too. In this book I will show you the benefits of the connection, how to make the connection, how to clear and heal the obstacles that come between you and your full, permanent connection, and how to accept and enjoy the power and freedom of being at one with your true spiritual self.

First, let's take a look at the powers that the connection to your Higher Self will bring you.

WHAT POWERS WILL YOU HAVE WHEN CONNECTED?

Your Higher Self is the pure spiritual essence of what you are and is created from divine source energy, so when you connect with it you have access to divine powers. These are:

✧ **The power of love.** You will have the ability to radiate and attract love without the fear of losing love, sabotaging relationships or driving away loving situations.

✧ **The power of wisdom.** You will be in touch with a source of knowledge that you are not aware of consciously but of which you yourself are a part. This knowledge is similar to a database that you connect to through your intuition and will supply you with inspiration and ideas, helping you to make choices that will benefit you.

✧ **The power of creation.** You will be able to manifest anything that you want, visualise and attract whatever you need. This is the divine power of creating form from thought. It will allow you to create positive and beneficial situations, rather than the destructive and challenging experiences that you may be going through now.

✧ **The power of purpose.** You will be in tune with your free will so that you choose what feels right for you, rather than being influenced by your fears or feelings of obligation, or by other people's attitudes.

✧ **The power of spirit.** Your psychic powers will be enhanced. This will improve your ability to heal and channel the energies of love, to be attuned to spirit and to the spiritual masters and angels that are there to help and guide you. You will be able to access the powers of inner sight, enabling you to see beyond the physical; inner audience, which will allow you to hear and communicate with spiritual beings such as angels; and telepathy, allowing you to communicate instinctively with friends and family. You will be aware of your spiritual connection to everyone and everything.

HOW WILL THESE POWERS HELP YOU IN YOUR DAILY LIFE AND WHAT WILL THEY GIVE YOU?

When you have received these powers, they will enable you:

✧ To be at ease with yourself and with your life – going with the flow instead of struggling.

✧ To be in control of the way you feel.

✧ To take the 'bad luck' out of your life.

✧ To handle without panic the challenges that life brings.

✧ To feel love and attract it into your life.

✧ To feel good about yourself and be happy.

✧ To be tolerant and understanding of yourself, in turn creating tolerance and understanding of those around you.

✧ To achieve a powerful connection to your intuition – knowing what is right for you.

✧ To live joyously with uplifted spirits, vitality and joie de vivre.

✧ To gain a sense of balance and harmony in your life.

✧ To gain a true understanding of how you create both the positive and negative aspects of your life.

✧ To enjoy the simple things in life without yearning for more all the time.

✧ To feel at one with nature.

✧ To find that creative pursuits flow with ease.

Being connected will affect you in whatever job or occupation you hold. Once you are healed and without fear and have found your right role, you will sense a feeling of being in the flow of your life. Here are just some examples of how it can be a benefit to you and your work:

✧ **In teaching** you will have a stronger empathy with the needs of your students. You will gain a sense of knowing what they can absorb and how to put over your subject most effectively.

✧ **In business** you will develop an intuitive sense of when to buy or sell, what your markets will accept, which employees to engage. You will find you have a strong sense of timing and a better understanding of your market and customers. Obstacles will not seem to be major disasters; they will no longer be a reason to become depressed or even give up, but a challenge that you can work through using your personal experience. Things go wrong even for the very best business magnates, but if your will and spirit is strong you will dust yourself off, learn from your mistakes and have another go.

✧ **As a mother.** If your role is to rear and support children you will find your connection invaluable. You will be able to take on the challenges of parenthood with patience and a deeper understanding of why your children react the way they do to any given situation. You will be able to fulfil their emotional needs as your own will not be in turmoil. You will be a perfect role model for them rather than an example of confusion, depression or even anger.

✧ **As a therapist.** All therapists and carers – in fact anyone working in any form of service – are potential healers, and your natural healing energies will become stronger and more powerful. You will be working from your heart and using your wisdom to react to the needs of others. Your connection to the energies of others will enable you to understand why they are the way they are, so that you can help them to heal and move on.

✧ **In a creative role.** You will be free of the blocks that beset any form of art or creativity. You will be in touch with the universal energies and able to flow with your work as never before.

WHAT I WILL BE SHARING WITH YOU

In the last two years I have been giving seminars to help other people make their own personal connection and achieve these same changes. Although my experience cannot be exactly replicated – trips to India come pretty expensive – I have developed a way that can help anyone who is ready to open up and reach up to take the major step of accepting and claiming their spirituality in its purest form. It has worked for my students, and in this book I will share this powerful process with you.

In each chapter I will take you through the same steps of the journey that I follow in my seminars, showing you how you can reconnect to your full personal spiritual power. In essence you need to raise the energy of your soul to the level of your Higher Self. To do this you will need to:

✧ Be aware of who you are and where you come from.

✧ Open yourself to giving and receiving love.

✧ Focus your intention to make the connection.

✧ Consciously integrate your heart, soul and divine presence.

✧ Positively see yourself as a harmonious, holistic being and heal and release all negativity.

✧ Believe in your ability to bring yourself back to your own divine self.

As I take you through these steps, each chapter will bring you closer to your goal, the continuous integration and connection of your soul with your divine self.

In Chapter 1 I will share my understanding of your spiritual aspect – your soul, your Higher Self, the source of creation – and how these relate and affect you. We will look at why you come to Earth, your life plan and the purpose of your existence.

In Chapter 2 we will look at the journey your soul takes; how you tick spiritually; what has caused your separation from your spiritual powers; why you may feel lonely, depressed, frustrated, confused and unloved.

In Chapter 3 I will show you how, using your own personal will and intention, you can dissolve the barriers between your soul and your Higher Self, allowing you to reconnect. I will share a powerful process that will allow you to make this connection and integration yourself.

In Chapter 4, as the journey continues, we will look at ways to bring balance and harmony into your life. We will see how your character, your ego, your physical, mental, emotional and spiritual aspects can affect each other, and how you can fuse these together to work co-operatively and harmoniously.

Next, in Chapter 5, we will look at negative energies, those thoughts and feelings that don't hold the high vibration of love and which will prevent you from being connected to your own higher state of love. I will show you how you can release this negativity that can affect your daily life: negativity caused by your fears, by reliving the past, by addictions or by other people's negative thoughts and fears.

In Chapter 6 I will show you how to clear guilt and karma, which are the greatest barriers between yourself and your self-esteem, your ability to feel worthy of the connection to your higher powers of spirit. Guilt can make you feel subconsciously that you don't deserve to be happy, driving a wedge between you and the Higher Self which is your 'happiness' aspect.

In Chapter 7 we will explore the setbacks, upsets, traumas, heartbreaks, put-downs, even domination by others, you may have experienced throughout your life. You may have lost a baby, a child, a lover, a dear friend or close family member through death or desertion. When traumatic and horrific events occur in your life your soul is affected. It holds the pain and affects the way you experience life from that moment on. In this chapter I will help you heal these wounds and restore the aspects of your personality and character that get lost when you suffer deeply. I will help you to heal and re-energise your soul, bringing it back to its greatest magnificence.

In Chapter 8, having healed the barriers that you have created due to past suffering and emotional pain, we can now work on creating a full and constant connection with your Higher Self, enabling you to integrate its energies and powers. I will help you to accept yourself as you are, and to accept also the divine aspect that is the core of your being. Through this acceptance you will be able to maintain your connection even when life throws up challenges and obstacles.

This then is the goal – to be fully connected all the time. Once you have achieved the connection you are on the way to full enlightenment. In this state you are totally immersed in love, with no fears, no anxieties, no bad feelings; fully content, at ease and at peace with yourself and the world. So in this book I will lead you through the healing of the scars from your past or your genetic inheritance, and help you to disperse the negativity from your own thoughts and those of others that can affect you every day. I will bring your entire being into a state of balance and harmony; bring you to a state of full integration with your original essence of pure love and creation.

WILL IT TAKE LONG AND IS IT HARD TO ACHIEVE?

Most transformations take time. I will guide you through a number of exercises that will enable you to set your own healing process in action. It will take a while for this process to counteract the habits and attitudes of a lifetime, but once your intention is set, things will start to change. When your consciousness is ready to believe that things can get better and that you can be healed, then you will start to see the results. The goal will be to believe that you are divine – I believe you are, but the major change will come to you when *you* believe you are. You may already know what I am telling you in this book, or you may know it at a deeper level. Once you accept the truth of my words, either by what you sense or by what you experience, then it will be anchored within you at a conscious level. Then the changes will manifest in how you feel and the amazing way in which life starts to open up for you.

Before I take you on your journey of reconnection, let me share with you a letter I received from a student of my seminars who has experienced the spiritual work I am presenting in this book:

Dear Anne,

I am so glad I attended your Healing Heart and Soul series of workshops. When we completed the final workshop I felt uplifted and positive. You helped me look inwards and examine how I have been functioning and it made me realise how negative and fearful I had become – how 'disconnected'. The work we did with you reinforced something I had always known but which had got overshadowed by my day-to-day worries and fears. That something was our divine connection, which is there regardless of what we go through. I now focus on this certainty and it has helped bring positivity back into my life. I now wake up and greet the day with gratitude, and look forward to the day ahead with joy and hope rather than with dread. There is no doubt that my life has begun to change for the better and positive things are beginning to happen. Thank you, Anne, for creating a safe and nurturing space to work in and for helping me move forward.

If this sounds good to you, come along and let's see how it's done. We will start by looking at the bigger picture of why we are here and where we come from.

ONE

The Source of Your Soul and its Journey

The first step towards a soul connection is to know who you are and your spiritual origins.

Before I tell you how you can claim your spiritual power I need to explain some fundamentals about your soul and its role in your life – how the physical you and the spiritual you integrate, and how you can relate to the greater consciousness that is all around you and in everything you see and feel. You need to be aware of why you are here and where you are going.

So here we go. The beginning seems to be a comfortable place to start! Let me give you my understanding of the conception and birth of your spiritual self and the long and, at times, difficult journey it has taken since. We will look at the purpose of life and the ultimate goal of your soul. We will also explore why you may feel so very alone at times, why life seems to be such a struggle and why things don't always work out the way that you would like.

GOD – SOURCE – GREATER CONSCIOUSNESS

Or even 'him upstairs'! You choose the name that best suits you. What I am referring to is the source of our creation; the source of the greatest love that can possibly be imagined; the creator of your soul and everything in the universe; an intelligent and loving force of love and light; the highest and most pure vibration of energy that flows through all of mankind, binding us together with a common thread of love and creational power. If you don't mind, I will call this magnificent energy 'God' – but he is not to be confused with the outdated vision of an old man with a white beard sitting on a cloud, waiting to hit us with a big stick whenever we do something wrong. The God I know is the source of an extraordinary flow of unconditional and non-judgemental love that flows down on us all at all times.

Unfortunately, the name of God has been hijacked and used as a way to personal power not necessarily for the benefit of all. The God I know uses only the power of love, a love that flows indiscriminately on to everyone whatever they have done, wherever they are on their journey, whatever their race, creed or culture. However, we are not all able to receive this love all the time – not because it is not shining on to us but because there are barriers between us and its source. I will explain why this occurs and what you can do about it. First let's see how your soul was conceived – what you were at the very beginning of your existence and how your journey has affected you since that innocent beginning.

The Source energy is supreme intelligence and infinite love, able to create from the intention of thought into matter. The energy of divine thought becomes the energy of form. In this way the universe was created – from divine intention and thought. The spiritual you was conceived in the same way. You started as a thought (no, not an idle thought!); you were intentionally created with a purpose in mind. This purpose has been with you since the very first moment your soul took off from its starting point and is your personal divine plan.

THE STARTING POINT

At the time of the Creation, when individual life and the galaxies were formed, God with thought and intention created a number of life forms to live in two areas or planes of existence. These planes are a big subject in themselves, but here I will simply refer to them as the higher and lower planes or dimensions. The higher planes are often referred to as Heaven and the vibration of their energy is high – so high that physical form does not exist in that rarefied and light atmosphere. In the higher planes energy exists as spirit only. In the lower planes, however, the energy is denser and heavier; here beings and things exist in a denser manner and can be seen as physical forms or material objects.

God created a number of beings whose energy was at a high level of vibration. These beings were helpers in the creation process and they live and exist on the higher planes. They are often referred to as Masters, Elohim or the gods of creation. These wise ones help us and guide us from the higher realms, and their assistance comes to us as thoughts, ideas and inspirations. Next to be created were the angels – both the great archangels such as Raphael, Uriel, Gabriel and Michael, and the smaller angels. There are different types of angels, but all have a purpose to oversee the world of humankind and to assist us whenever we need help. They fulfil their roles from the higher dimensions of existence and are rarely to be seen in physical form.

It's important at this point to emphasise that everything that is created comes from the thought of the being we call God or Source. This is divine energy and can create form or matter from thought. The energy to make these new forms of existence also derived from this same source of divine energy. This means that everything was created from the high vibration energy of love. This is what God is – LOVE.

CREATING MONADS AND SOULS

Now we come to the interesting part – the part that is about us. God put out the intention, put out the thought, of creating a life form that could exist on the lower planes but still be connected to Source. In other words Source created a separate part of itself that could travel and experience things. This energy form we call a monad. It is a smaller version of Source, of God. It has the same attributes as God and is created from the Source energy, so it is made of love and is capable of creating matter from thought and intention. But it also holds an intention of being – a purpose. Many monads have been created, each with a slightly different purpose, for the development of the consciousness of Source. In other words, their role is to take love and creation down to lower dimensions where the energy is denser and form and matter exist – our realm of Earth.

These various purposes held by different monads all hold the light in some way or other. In terms of modern life, you might visualise a monad for doctors and caring for the physical needs of humanity, a monad to bring light in the business world as leaders or as financial managers or through production, and so on. As the world has developed and evolved, so the roles have been modified to suit each age, but the underlying purpose will stay through every lifetime the monad experiences on Earth. This purpose is called the blueprint of purpose or your personal divine plan, and will be the focus of every life you experience.

Monadic energy never loses its original state of unconditional love or its pure unblemished form of divine energy. That means the monad energy cannot in itself come down to Earth, because here it will experience dense and negative energies that will take it away from its state of pure love. So the monad subdivides itself into a number of unique units each with its own consciousness, each with a special calling within its overall purpose. Each of these units is a unique being, just like you and me.

So your spiritual aspect has two parts:

✧ The Higher Self – which stays with the monad and permanently holds the energy of love.

✧ The soul – which travels down to Earth and is incarnated with a physical form.

These two parts are connected by a silver cord. This is a spiritual energy cord that connects your soul both to your Higher Self and, while you are alive, to your body.

The purpose of the soul is to experience the trials and tribulations of a life on Earth – the lower dimension. Although your soul is spiritual energy created of love, it can be wounded and damaged by the experiences of earthly life. For example betrayal, great grief or guilt are all experiences that can damage your soul.

You can see how this looks in the illustration. See how

the energy of Source continually flows down to the monad and soul. This means that the soul can receive a constant flow of love and healing.

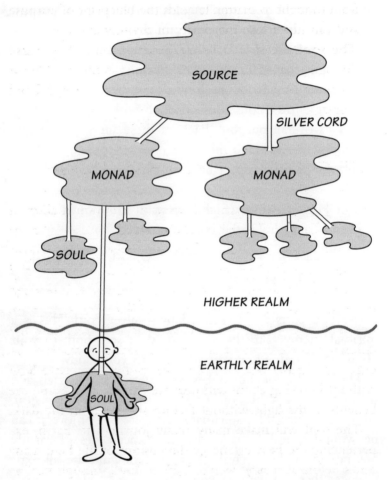

Source, monad and soul

Let's just confirm the three spiritual states of divine love that flow to us as individuals:

1. **Source/God**, *created of divine love*, holds the wisdom of everything created, and has the power to create from thought to matter.
2. **The monad**, *created of divine love*, has the power to create from thought to matter. It holds the blueprint of purpose and can never lose the purity of divinity and love.
3. **The soul**, *created of divine love*, holds the monad's purpose through journeys to Earth. It can be wounded by what it experiences on its journeys to Earth's lower realm and dense dimension.

THE CYCLE OF BIRTH AND DEATH

So Source creates monads and monads create souls, all from the same energy of love. This is the essential key to who we are – the source of all our existence is therefore divine love. However, the soul journeys down to Earth, which is of a lower vibration and where love is not constant. It is through these journeys to Earth that the soul learns to cope with love and lack of love. In other words it finds out about the difference between light and dark, it learns about love by experiencing the lack of it. For we cannot appreciate light without knowing about darkness, we cannot understand the benefits of the light without feeling and being in the dark.

The soul will make many, many journeys to Earth, experiencing the heavier energy dimensions of life here many times before it finally evolves back to love, through healing and spiritual endeavour. Only then can it return to Source and finish its cycle of life and death. During its journeys the soul will have many painful experiences that will create pain felt through the mind, emotions and physical body, and some of these painful episodes will cause deep wounds. However, no matter what happens to the soul on its journey, your higher/monadic self will always hold the pure energy of divine love. In Chapter 2 I will explain in more detail how these wounds can appear to separate your soul from its monad or Higher Self.

Your soul joins your physical form at the time of your birth. This is when you become a being that is both spiritual and physical. Let's look now at how these two major aspects of you unite and interface with each other.

LINKING SPIRITUAL AND PHYSICAL

We are therefore two parts – physical and spiritual. These two aspects are linked together through a number of energy centres that allow the energies to flow between the physical you and the spiritual you. They also act as conduits for emotions and feelings and can have a strong influence on how you feel from moment to moment. We will see later how they affect your general wellbeing, particularly your ability to be open to love. These energy centres are often called chakras – which means spinning wheel in Sanskrit – and take the form of vortices of spinning energy. The illustration shows these energy centres and where they sit on the physical body.

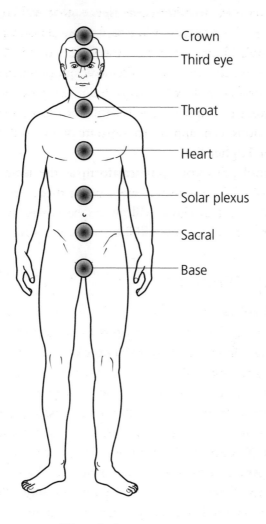

Crown

Third eye

Throat

Heart

Solar plexus

Sacral

Base

The chakra positions

YOUR LIFE PLAN

As your soul prepares for each life journey it will reside in the higher dimensions. Here you will plan your next lifetime with help from the elders and Masters. There will be lessons that you want to learn, aspects of yourself you want to heal, knowledge you wish to acquire and missions that you wish to complete. Each life will be different but every life will be affected by your monadic purpose, your divine plan. If this purpose is to give service and help others, then that will be the overriding purpose of each lifetime. Any lesson that you have not learnt from previous journeys to Earth will be repeated as part of your plan. This repeating of experiences may seem to create a pattern of behaviour – for example, if you cannot learn to forgive then you will find that an opportunity will always be created for you to forgive, which means you will suffer from the words or actions of others.

However, as you are born, as your soul binds with your physical foetal form, your memory of the past disappears. It will still be there at the level of your Higher Self/monad, but your conscious mind will forget both what has happened in past lives and what plan you have made for the life ahead. This might seem a bit hard – it certainly causes us many challenges – but if you knew what was to come you would behave in a totally different manner and the choices you make would be influenced by your expectation of the outcome. You would take short cuts and deliberately avoid confrontation, neither of which would test and challenge you sufficiently to gain the experience and fulfil the purpose of a life journey on earth.

So your life plan acts as your blueprint – the ideal way for you to live each life. It holds your original intention and purpose, as given to you and agreed with God on your soul's conception. It holds the guidelines and intention for this lifetime just like a route map for your journey. As you have free will, when you are on Earth you can change your plan at any time. But the ideal route is sitting with your Higher

Self – so the more connected with your Higher Self you are, the more likely it is that you will find the easy route through life.

A STOREHOUSE OF WISDOM

Although you forget what has happened in past lives, the knowledge you have gleaned from your different lifetimes is stored at your monadic level as part of your Higher Self. This database of past experiences and lessons learned is like a huge library which is available to you at any time and is often referred to as your causal body. Some people are more in touch with this than others – which explains why some people can speak foreign languages more easily than others, why we sometimes have a sense of déjà vu when we visit a new place and why we can have skills and abilities that are superior to those of other family members – why, for example, a genius can play music without ever having been taught.

We will tap into much of the wisdom we hold at this higher level through our intuition. Your intuitive ability reflects how connected you are to the database of stored wisdom at your monadic level. Psychics can tap into your causal body when they look to see what has happened to cause your current problems. I can see the past life experiences of my clients, whether they are with me or on the phone, because I can see into their causal body where everything that has ever happened to them is stored. Through your life journey you can get in touch with your higher wisdom through your intuition, an ability that develops as you become more fully connected to your higher (monadic) self.

You are probably now getting a better picture of why it's important to be connected.

As you become more connected you will start to make choices that suit your character, your past experience and your skills and abilities.

CHOOSING WHO WILL HELP YOU

You also get a lot of help on your journey. Before you come down to Earth you will make plans to meet up and inter-face with different souls who have travelled with you in past lives and with whom you have a connection and affinity. These souls that are special to you are called soul mates. They may assist you or challenge you in any particular life, but either way they will help you to learn your chosen lessons for that lifetime.

THE ROLE OF SOUL MATES

So, having arranged to meet up, you will have experiences that include certain of these soul mates. You will not neces-sarily plan to meet, fall in love and live happily ever after. You may for example ask a soul mate to challenge you on a perceived weakness in order to see if you can overcome it and become stronger. Perhaps you have allowed others to dominate you in previous lives, so in this lifetime a soul mate may be a bully in the school playground, giving you a chance to stand up to domineering attitudes and behaviour. Or a soul mate may be a beggar who tests your compassion, or a difficult neighbour who teaches you tolerance and patience. On the other hand your soul mate may be a partner to give you support and love through your life as a parent, sibling, friend, business colleague or lover. Whatever role your soul mates play will be part of your plan, and they will be there to help you. So now you can look at your mother-in-law in a different light!

Let me share how a soul mate has helped me to grow though both negative and positive actions. I am married to one of my soul mates, Tony. We met when we were in our twenties, but after a while he left me, leaving me broken-hearted. This was a repeat of a past life experience, although at that time I was unaware of this. I dusted myself off and threw myself into my work, and managed to make myself independent and happy without him. I didn't feel the need for another permanent relationship. Eventually however I met him again, fifteen years later, and we fell in love again and married. How romantic!

I realise now that this was a great test for me, for in a previous lifetime I had been devastated by his departure and found myself unable to be happy without him. My attach-ment was so strong that I depended completely on him for my happiness. It seems he was unhappy about the amount of time I spent on my work – I probably neglected him. For several lifetimes I would not allow myself to have any liaisons, for I felt unable to trust and my heart was closed. I put all my resources and attention into my work as a healer and spiritual teacher. I felt that I couldn't have my work and a lover too. I learnt to live alone and make myself happy without a constant companion, which proved to be a great lesson for me and helped to make me stronger.

In this lifetime I love Tony and have had a wonderful life with him, but I have also completed my contract to do my healing work. I have proved to myself that I can be happy when we are apart, for his work has taken him away for long periods. I ensure that he gets plenty of my attention, while I have managed to balance my life so that I can do my work and also have a normal loving relationship. In fact I can have it all!

WILL I RECOGNISE A SOUL MATE IF I MEET HIM OR HER?

This is a question I am often asked. Most likely you will feel something. You may be immediately attracted to someone without understanding why. They may not fit the prototype of your typical lover or have the character that normally attracts you as a friend or partner but you still feel drawn to them. If your soul mate is a difficult neighbour or domineering mother you may not allow yourself to open up to them, but if you do you may see through the illusion of their behaviour. You may find that you become reconciled once you have learnt the tolerance or ability to stand up for yourself or whatever is relevant for your lesson.

CHOOSING THE RIGHT TIME AND PLACE

I am often asked about astrology and what role it has to play in our life plan and the situations that occur in our lives. So I will take a moment here to give you my understanding of the role played in our overall plan by the planets. In further preparation for your coming journey to Earth, you will choose the best time and situation both for your birth and all the major events that you wish to experience. An important part of your life plan is the planetary positions at the time of your birth, for these will have a powerful influence on the challenges and fortune you will attract in your life. The energy of the planets and their influences on each other will affect not only what comes your way but also your personality and character – the part of you that interfaces with the world. The constellation you choose for the time of your birth will depend on the opportunities and challenges on which you need to be tested in your life.

A good reading of your chart can give you deep insights into who you are and the role you are here to play. From the time that you are born your plan for a particular lifetime will be held in the constellation of planets, as will the possibilities and probabilities for situations to unfurl at certain times in your life. In your quest to get to know yourself better you may find it helpful to have a chart drawn up by a competent astrologer. You can use it not just to see what is coming but to gain perspective on what has happened in your past and the gifts and abilities that you bring with you. You will see that you gain certain characteristics from the position of the planets, and from their relationships with each other and with the moon. Your personality and character traits will either help you to move smoothly through your life and make easy relationships, if you are charismatic, open or loving, or bring up challenges if you are prickly and over-sensitive or pushy and dominant. Either way it will have all been part of your plan and your choice.

My own chart reflects virtually all my aspects and my approach to life. Although I am a Capricorn my chart is influenced by Sagittarius, which indicates that I will spend a great deal of my life travelling. This is true, as I have always needed to feel free and travel – when I was younger I was restless and wanted to be out and about, I felt that life was passing me by while I spent time indoors. Since my mid-twenties I have travelled with my work and now I do so more than ever!

Your chart will give you an indication what is the most important purpose of your current lifetime – what your soul feels you need to heal or master in order to be able to expand and grow. For me, in order to realise the absolute necessity that I should make my own decisions and control my own destiny with freedom, I had to have a conflict with someone who wanted to restrain and control me. Now I am with a partner who allows me total freedom. I will stop before I give all my secrets away, but I cannot stress enough how a good reading will help you understand who you are and explain why certain events have occurred. Remember – you created your plan and chose the influences that would affect you in your life.

To get the best out of a reading from the point of view of healing your soul, I suggest that you ask your astrologer to focus on your past and the influences it is having on your present situation, rather than just telling you of your future. Your chart will also help you know yourself, an important step in your journey of understanding why you are the way you are. I must admit that in the past I dismissed the influence of planetary positions and the power of astrology, and only used it to see what the future held. However, I have recently found deep and meaningful insights in my own readings that have clarified a great deal about my behaviour and why some of my endeavours have been more successful than others. So I suggest you may like to delve more deeply into the impact your star signs have on your personality and character traits.

Here are some very broad characteristics indicated by the twelve star signs, as mentioned in the on-line Wikipedia encyclopaedia. I have included some of the more negative trends, and you may like to see if there is anything there that you can work on! Due to other influences, either those in your life or your past or in the effects of other planetary positions – such as the position of the Moon and the way the planets are lined up – many of these traits may not occur in your own make-up, so I do recommend you get a personalised reading for a more accurate picture. I have given details of my recommended astrologer in the Resources section at the back of the book.

Sagittarius: Keyword 'I philosophise'
Freedom loving, extrovert, straightforward, benevolent, philosophical, idealistic, sincere, intellectual, knowledgeable, broad-minded, truth-seeking, fun-loving, athletic, adventurous, expansive and optimistic. Can be blundering, careless, exaggerative, know-it-all, over-indulgent, tactless and scattered. Ruled by Jupiter. Sun sign dates: 22 November–21 December.

Capricorn: Keyword 'I use'
Prudent, responsible, realistic, formal, patient, methodical, disciplined. Traditional, cautious, conventional, hard-working, persevering, self-reliant, ambitious, businesslike, career-oriented, authoritative, conscientious and competent. Can be rigid, suspicious, status-seeking, demanding, insensitive and inhibited. Ruled by Saturn. Sun sign dates: 22 December–20 January.

Aquarius: Keyword 'I know'
Unconventional, detached, intellectual, objective, individualistic, inventive, tolerant, unique, rebellious, sophisticated, future-oriented, humanitarian, cause-oriented, believes in groups and society, progressive. Can be dogmatic, unpredictable, over-permissive, aloof, eccentric and elitist. Ruled by Saturn and Uranus. Sun sign dates: 21 January–19 February.

Pisces: Keyword 'I believe'
Compassionate, empathetic, imaginative, sensitive, mystical, spiritual, dreamy, passive, easy-going, idealistic, visionary, inspirational, accepting, undiscriminating, charitable, believes in soul growth, self-sacrificing and artistic. Can be distracted, detached, illusory, impractical, gullible, neglectful, escapist and lazy. Ruled by Jupiter and Neptune. Sun sign dates: 20 February–20 March.

Aries: Keyword 'I am'
Assertive, brave, energetic, action-oriented, intelligent, individualistic, independent, impulsive, full of strength, competitive, eager, straightforward, forceful, headstrong, pioneering, a leader, focused on the present and freedom-loving. Can be intemperate, violent, impatient, fiery, rash, extreme and arrogant. Ruled by Mars and Pluto. Sun sign dates: 21 March–20 April.

Taurus: Keyword 'I have'
Resourceful, thorough, dependable, responsible, loyal, patient, placid, stable, sensual, affectionate, comfortable, solid, earthy, strong, money-oriented, practical, productive, cautious, musical and artistic. Can be stubborn, indulgent, insecure, acquisitive, possessive, rigid, stodgy and slow. Ruled by Venus. Sun sign dates: 21 April–21 May.

Gemini: Keyword 'I think'
Versatile, inquisitive, whimsical, nimble, articulate, lively, active, curious, talkative, sociable, mercurial. Can be restless, scattered, dual or two-faced, inconstant, gullible, gossipy and superficial. Ruled by Mercury. Sun sign dates: 22 May–21 June.

Cancer: Keyword 'I feel'
Protective, sensitive, tenacious, retentive, resourceful, self-contained, family and home oriented, maternal, security-oriented, nurturing, warm, sympathetic, patriotic, sentimental, emotional and loving. Can be touchy, clinging, over-protective, moody and crabby. Ruled by the Moon. Sun sign dates: 22 June–23 July.

Leo: Keyword 'I will'
Creative, generous, proud, risk-taking, fun-loving, dramatic, dignified, theatrical, passionate, affectionate, ardent, ambitious, loves attention, independent, noble, a leader, sunny, bright, magnetic, kingly, powerful. Can be bossy, patronising, snobbish, egotistical, boastful, over self-conscious and arrogant. Ruled by the Sun. Sun sign dates: 24 July–23 August.

Virgo: Keyword 'I analyse'
Practical, industrious, efficient, thorough, methodical, exacting, precise, detail-oriented, observant, critical, work and service oriented, painstaking, pragmatic, modest, discreet, health and cleanliness conscious, mentally active and flexible. Can be fussy, nervous, pedantic, petty and over-critical. Ruled by Mercury. Sun sign dates: 24 August–22 September.

Libra: Keyword 'I balance'
Co-operative, diplomatic, sees both sides, open-minded, just, urbane, fair, partnership oriented, avoids conflict, refined, balanced, graceful, charming, debative, idealistic, equalitarian and sociable. Can be easily deterred, indecisive and lazy. Ruled by Venus. Sun sign dates: 23 September–23 October.

Scorpio: Keyword 'I desire'
Passionate, secretive, powerful, penetrating, intense, determined, purposeful, keenly perceptive, deep, complex, analytical, inquisitive, resourceful, ambitious, magnetic, hypnotic, sexual, creative and mysterious. Can be cunning, suspicious, compulsive, aggressive, jealous and controlling. Ruled by Mars and Pluto. Sun sign dates: 24 October–21 November.

IF MY BIRTH WAS INDUCED WHAT EFFECT CAN THAT HAVE ON MY STAR SIGNS?

I believe that even the fact that your doctor induced you on Friday because he wanted to play golf on Saturday is part of your plan! I don't believe in accidents and happenstance. I believe that virtually everything is considered. Certain times in your life are quite critical and you have a choice whether to take the opportunities that arrive at those times or let them pass, but the overall plan will follow its course despite what seem to be accidents.

CAN I MAKE CHANGES TO MY LIFE PLAN DURING MY LIFETIME?

When you are born you are given an outstanding gift, one that you bring to Earth with you. That is the gift of free will and the ability to make your own choices. In other words, you are not programmed simply to follow the blueprint that you set out for any particular lifetime. All roads lead you eventually to your enlightenment – the state in which you are once more filled with light and love – so there are no wrong paths, no wrong decisions. Of course, there will be decisions that may take you on a rockier road, but you will get there in the end.

Before you are reconnected consciously to your Higher Self, you may find that you make certain decisions based on desire or fear. Once you become connected, your intuition will be in touch with your higher wisdom and therefore you will be more inclined to make choices that suit you emotionally, mentally, physically and spiritually. The closer you are to your soul and your monad, the greater chance that you will know what you truly want for your highest good. So, yes, you can decide to do something that wasn't part of your original plan.

THE JOURNEY'S END

Your soul will stay with your body through thick and thin throughout your lifetime and it is only released to travel back to its monad at the time of your death. As your physical body expires, so your soul energy rises up and leaves your body to follow the silver cord back to your monad. It will stay in the higher planes until such time as you choose to return for further experiences and adventures.

So your journey is plotted and planned and your destiny to a certain extent is laid down. However, you do have free will, and it's important to know that the journey you take and the lessons you have come to learn can be filled with love or filled with fear. It's you that decides which. Remember that your goal is to raise your soul's energy vibration to that of your monad, bringing yourself back to a state of love without scars and wounds, fears and guilt.

Now we have seen where our spiritual aspect comes from and what is its purpose, we will look at how we sense a separation from our divine source, our monad, and become disconnected from our Higher Self and its love.

TWO

Separation from Your Higher Self

The separation of your soul from your divine self is the greatest tragedy that befalls your soul in its journey to Earth. Fortunately, you have the power to reconnect.

In this chapter I will show you how and why you have become separated from your Higher Self and look at what effects this separation can have on your life. I will then be your guide for the journey back home to end the separation and become united again with your Higher Self and your spiritual powers.

As I have explained, the purpose of your soul is to come to Earth and learn the lessons of light and love, and to overcome the challenges of loss of love and the emotional wounding that this loss causes. These challenges and their outcomes create the illusion that you are separated from the constant stream of love that comes from Source and have lost touch with the energy of your Higher Self. As you experience these lessons you may move further and further away from the state of high vibrational energy of love in which you were created. This means you are going to lose your awareness of and contact with your monad. In other words you will not consciously be connected to your monad, although in fact your silver cord will still be connecting you.

As you become denser and your energy becomes heavier, you will no longer remember that you are divine. You may have hundreds of lifetimes full of lessons before you start to come back and begin to remember that you are light, that you are created from love. But eventually you will remember and acknowledge who you are, and then you will regain the state of enlightenment. Enlightenment means you are once more full of love and can regain full access to your Higher Self and to God. When you reach enlightenment your energy is of the highest vibration, the same vibration as your monad. In other words you are again fully pure divine love. Once you become enlightened you no longer need to continue your cycle of birth and death on Earth. Your soul can return to the monad and you can stay in the higher realms of existence, generally known as Heaven, Paradise or Nirvana – a place of great beauty where all spirit lives in harmony and joy.

Let's now look in more detail at how this drop of energy from love and light occurs; how you become separated from the knowledge of who you are.

MOVING AWAY FROM UNCONDITIONAL LOVE

When your soul came on its first journey to Earth it was full of unconditional love. It joined your chosen earthly body at the time of physical conception and became at one with that physical body. You, as body and soul, became a person of spirit and form, ready to face earthly life for the first time.

During that first life you will have had some experience

of love and most likely some experience of loss of love, either through rejection or the death of a loved one. On these lower, earthly planes love becomes corrupted by attachment, possessiveness and insecurity. We worry about losing our loved ones and forget that our soul continues its journey even when the body dies. These insecurities about love affect the way we treat each other. We learn about anger and emotional pain. We start to experience the pain when love is withdrawn and we turn that pain outwards in an attempt to heal it. This creates a cycle of getting hurt and hurting others. It also sets in motion the law of karma, the spiritual law that governs our actions of cause and effect. What you do to others will come back to you and you will begin to feel the burden of guilt, which is the pain of karma.

You will also learn to shut out love. When you received your first setback with love you felt severe pain in your heart centre, the energy centre linking your emotions and physical body, which is found in the middle of your chest (see the illustration on p. 21). Your heart centre controls the giving and receiving of love. It will be damaged by severe loss and it holds the pain that we call grief. To help you cope with the hurting inside you may shut the door of your heart to avoid further pain.

Your entire being is surrounded by an energy field (aura) that reflects your emotional, mental and spiritual state. Once you start to feel these emotional pains your energy field will start to drop into a heavier vibration. At that point you have started the separation of yourself, of your soul, from its monad – your Higher Self. For as your energy vibration changes from the highest frequency of love and you start to hold the lower frequencies of fear, grief and guilt, so you will drift away from your state of divine, unconditional love. As you go through more and more lifetimes, so you will drift further and further apart from your true essence and the sense of connection to God will fade. This separation causes you even more pain, for you feel alone and unloved, far from the greatest source of love that there is.

The next illustration will help you to see what happens. The layers of pain and hurt act as a barrier between you and your Higher Self, creating a sense of isolation and aloneness. This is how you lose that wonderful feeling of being part of a bigger being, part of all that which is God.

The separation
Wounds and guilt and loss of love create the
barriers and sense of separation.

OUTCOMES OF THE SEPARATION

As you lose touch with your origins, with your Higher Self, with God and the true essence of who you are, you are likely to feel a sense of isolation. The energies of love are continually flowing towards you but you don't feel or acknowledge them. It is difficult to heal when you don't receive love and it's difficult to feel spiritually uplifted from day to day when you are isolated from God. Here are some of the symptoms you may experience through your separation:

✧ Feelings of loneliness and isolation from the rest of the world.

✧ A sense of abandonment – nobody cares and you are unwanted.

✧ A feeling of being an outcast, different from other people.

✧ Confusion about the purpose of life.

✧ A tendency to depression and mood swings.

✧ A sense of being driven to reach some elusive goal.

✧ A feeling of being let down in some way – that life is not what it could be.

✧ A sense that although you may feel happy at times, constant happiness is unobtainable whatever you do.

✧ A lack of fulfilment.

✧ A sense that you are carrying the burden of other people's cares and responsibilities alone, without the help of God and spirit.

✧ Inner fears and anxieties plague you – even panic attacks with no real cause.

✧ Chronic illness or a constant feeling of being unwell.

✧ Difficulty in meeting someone who understands and loves you.

✧ Difficulties with relationships, feeling misunderstood.

✧ Inner anger that wells up and destroys relationships.

✧ Difficulty in manifesting the things you want in life.

✧ Uncertainty about your life's purpose and what you are here to do.

✧ A feeling that you are a victim of life.

✧ Intolerance of yourself and others – always striving for elusive perfection.

✧ Everything you do is a struggle – you work hard but success still eludes you.

✧ Feelings of insecurity; inability to gain permanent financial stability or support.

✧ A belief that life means suffering – that everyone has to get sick at some time.

✧ Bitterness about the hand you have been dealt – life seems unfair.

✧ Crying and becoming emotional for no apparent reason.

✧ Feelings of guilt that won't go away despite all the work you do.

✧ A need to please others to such an extent that your own health and happiness suffers.

✧ Complete lack of confidence in yourself – you focus on your perceived weakest points.

These and others are all symptoms of your separation from your highest spiritual state, your Higher Self.

The further you move from the energies of love, the less you are in alignment with your Higher Self, the more intense these feelings of separation will become.

WHAT CAN I DO ABOUT SEPARATION?

Remember that it's not your fault that this separation is happening. Such feelings are a direct result of your negative experiences; they are caused by the heavy energy that you and others carry while down on the Earth plane. Every time you upset someone or they upset you the separation will become greater. What's more, the effects are cumulative from one lifetime to the next. You bring the baggage of previous lives with you when you arrive. These affect how you act and behave towards others, and how other people receive and treat you. We will look further into this and how you can heal and release these old scars in the following chapters, so don't give up hope. There is a way out of this cycle, a way to close the gap and end the separation.

To look on the bright side and to help you to become motivated, let's look at some of the things that achieving your goal of being fully connected and acknowledging your own divinity will give you:

✧ A sense of calm at all times, even when those around you are in turmoil.

✧ Knowing who you are and what your role in life is.

✧ Total acceptance of yourself – warts and all.

✧ Tolerance and understanding of those around you.

✧ A powerful connection to your intuition – knowing what is right for you.

✧ A sense of empathy and connection to all of life.

✧ The ability to see the good in everyone, including yourself.

✧ The ability to draw towards you all that you need – people, opportunities, finance, etc.

✧ A feeling of happiness and contentment.

✧ A sense of ease – life will no longer be a struggle.

✧ The capacity to live joyously with uplifted spirits and joie de vivre.

✧ An inner glow that radiates from you, affecting everyone you meet.

✧ A sense of balance and harmony in your life.

✧ An understanding of other people and the ability to be discerning about those you wish to share your life with.

✧ A true understanding that you create your own life.

✧ The ability to enjoy the simple things in life without yearning for more all the time.

✧ A feeling of oneness with nature.

✧ An understanding of yourself and your reactions to situations and people.

✧ A sense of your connection to God, and the ability to
feel the energies of love that flow from Source.

✧ Creative pursuits will flow with ease.

I took Molly through the process of integration some time
ago. Here is how it affected her:

My journey following integration

*I have more focus, direction and clarity and can now deal with
and transform any negative energies that come into my life,
and which would have seriously challenged me before.*

*I am in touch now with a clear, strong belief in my Higher
Self. When I called on my Higher Self with clear intention I
felt a strong movement from my heart and could see the spirit
of my Higher Self looking me straight in the eyes. It was a
moment of true awakening and acknowledgement, a truly
powerful sensation, and I felt my Higher Self say 'Acknowledge
me and work with me. I AM is the strength within. I come
from within and now return within. I am part of you, even
as your breath. I am your soul, trust me.' I felt so free, light
and powerful. I see everything with more light now and see
the clarity and beauty in all. I feel the difference between imagination and true connection – a pure feeling divorced from ego.*

*I have a feeling of clairvoyance with passed loved ones and
with those around me. Especially I can hear the 'voice' of
animals. Since I connected my work has increased and owners
are bringing their animals to me for healing – I am sure this
is no coincidence. Doors are now opening and the direction of
my life and work is more defined.*

I no longer feel alone with my spiritual journey. Instead I feel supported from within and know it is my own special god-given power which is giving me more communication with angels and Ascended Masters. I now work with Spirit and my I AM energy.

Remember who you are - a spiritual being in physical form.

THE MAJOR STEPS TO BECOMING RECONNECTED

There are six major stages to completing and holding the connection with your Higher Self and totally integrating your highest spiritual aspect. You will need to work on these over and over again to ensure a full and complete connection. As you work through these steps you will find that you connect some of the time and some of the time you will stray. Your connection will wax and wane; it will fluctuate, sometimes day by day, depending on what is going on around you and within you. But keep working at it. We will look later at ways that you can heal the deeper wounds that may be hindering a full connection. Don't give up. Eventually you will definitely get it!

Go through this process, holding the intention of creating a full and lasting connection, and you will most likely find immediate benefits and changes. Eventually, when the connection is complete and sustained, your powers of manifesting, creating, attracting and feeling totally at peace and one with the world will be with you full time.

✧ Stage one   Remember you are divine

✧ Stage two   Open your heart

✧ Stage three Intend to end the separation

✧ Stage four   Integrate your heart, soul and divine presence

✧ Stage five   Release all negativity and heal all wounds of
               your soul

✧ Stage six   Believe it and enjoy it!

I will now lead you through the first three stages to prepare you for your reconnection and integration. Afterwards, in Chapter 4, I will take you through the powerful integration process. In the following chapters, we will see how you can release the imbalance in your life and clear the negativity and wounds that have caused the separation. Then, in the final chapter, we will see how you can believe in and accept your integration. You can repeat any or all these steps as many times as you like. Some of what follows will seem strange to start with – it may be new to your belief system. It may wake up old memories, so you may experience emotional upsets. But keep at it, for once you start the process life will never be the same again.

   To prepare yourself for your planned reconnection and integration, we'll start by working on stages one to three. I suggest you do these exercises several times to anchor within you the intention to make the connection and prepare your energy for the shift that will occur when you achieve integration.

REMEMBER YOU ARE DIVINE

Now is the time to recognise and accept that you are a spiritual being living in physical form. Through many spiritual and enlightening experiences, I have come to understand this aspect of myself and it has transformed my life. I feel immeasurably better about myself, about my life and the people I share it with, about society in general. I have changed my perception of what life is about and it has made everything much, much more comfortable, easy and fun. I no longer have to struggle not to surrender to a low state of mind and body; instead I am attuned to a higher and more elevated one. I feel in tune with life and am creating what I want as I go along.

This is how I would like everyone to feel. It hasn't taken anything very difficult. I haven't had to give up the things I love in life. I still have a drink, enjoy new clothes, have holidays, have a normal family life (if there is such a thing!); I am a perfectly ordinary grounded woman. But I appreciate and acknowledge who I am. So the first step to take is to allow the concept of being spiritual to sit with you. I hope I have explained your connection to spirit, but let me just reconfirm what integration is and what it will do for you.

In your lifetimes on Earth you have faced a number of challenges. You have been seduced by desires; you have been drawn from the path of honesty and integrity; you have been betrayed, abandoned and abused; you have found and lost love; you have made promises to other souls, to God and yourself; you have broken some of these promises. You have acquired great skills, wisdom and understanding about the world, other people and yourself. You have learnt what makes you feel good and what upsets you. You have followed your path and destiny in the best way you can. All these experiences have allowed you to grow spiritually, but many of them have left you wounded, guilty and often out of balance and harmony.

The purpose of the integration is to initiate the beginning of the shift to spiritual enlightenment and fulfilment. Through reconnection to your divine self you can again have access to divine powers. This will mean that life works for you and with you instead of against you. Through your integration and acceptance of yourself as divine you will have full access to God and the divine powers of the universe and all of creation. When you are fully connected to the powers of the Divine there is no limit to what you can achieve; no limit to the love you can give and receive; no limit to your physical and spiritual powers. You will be able to manifest everything you need. You will be able to use telepathy to communicate and much, much more. All these will come in time; in the short term you will feel more at ease with yourself and enjoy your life without struggle.

Remember:

✧ You are divine because you are created from divine energy.

✧ You are love because you are created from the energy of love.

✧ You are a creator because you were created from the energy of creation.

✧ You are a spirit living in a physical body.

DAILY MANTRA

A mantra is an affirmation that you say out loud to reinforce your mind and consciousness of a new concept and a change of belief. Below is a mantra that will help to remind you that you are divine. Set aside some time to say this every day. I suggest you repeat it at least 100 times before performing the integration process. Say it aloud when you are alone and repeat it in your mind when you have other people around you, whenever you have a moment.

'I am a spiritual being in a physical body, I am divine and created from pure love. I am love.'

OPEN YOUR HEART

To receive the love that will flow from your Higher Self your heart needs to be open. Not your physical heart but your emotional and spiritual heart, the centre of energy that is located in the middle of your chest and governs the giving and receiving of love. Even if you have opened your heart to give, it may be closed to receive. You may have been hurt by someone who has withdrawn their love, either deliberately or through death, and this can break your heart. This deep and painful wounding of your heart centre is where we get the term 'heartbreak'. The energy wheel of your heart chakra, which allows the flow of love, can actually be torn and the pain can be palpable – as real as any physical pain. I consider healing and opening your heart so important that I wrote the book *Opening Your Heart*, in which I focus on all the different situations that can cause heart wounds and how you can relieve and heal them. If you have any reason to believe that your heart is closed, then I suggest you read that book as soon as you can, for it will guide you to open your heart to receive love.

HOW DO I KNOW IF MY HEART IS CLOSED?

There are clues and symptoms that will let you know whether your heart is closed. Here are some of them:

✧ You find it difficult to have close relationships.

✧ You fear being rejected.

✧ You fear that others are critical of you.

✧ You feel you must please others all the time.

✧ You sense you will never meet the right person for you.

You may well have a heart that is partially closed, as I had, and not be aware of it. I recommend that you go through the following heart-opening exercise, for it will reinforce your intention to be clear of old grief and open to love. If your heart is closed due to past pain that you associate with love, if you have barriers in place to prevent this pain occurring again, if you are not open to receive, then you will be shutting yourself off not only from the love that comes from a lover, friend, parent or child but from the joys of life itself. You will be cutting yourself off from divine love and the healing that it brings. There is a very high chance that your soul is wounded in some way from a past traumatic experience, either in this lifetime or a previous one; otherwise you would not have returned to Earth for this life.

Your soul needs love to heal.

Your soul cannot flourish without love. It needs to heal the past hurt that has come from betrayal, abuse, abandonment, cruelty and guilt. To receive love you need to have your heart open, therefore you need to open your heart to receive healing for your soul.

Visualisation to open your heart

Here is a simple visualisation you can use to help your heart to start to open. Later in this book I will offer you other ways to heal. There are also further techniques in *Opening Your Heart* (see Recommended Reading at the back of this book):

✧ Find a quiet and secluded place without phones or inter-ruptions. Sit or lie comfortably and close your eyes.

✧ Breathe in deeply four times. Count to three on each breath. Know you are breathing in healing energies of love on the in-breath and letting go old grief and pain on the out-breath.

✧ Visualise yourself as a great oak tree and see your roots growing down deep, deep into the earth. You are now grounded and stabilised.

✧ Put your hand on your heart centre in the middle of your chest. Say out loud *'I open my heart to give and receive love.'* Repeat twice.

✧ Visualise a beautiful door opening wide. Say *'I release all pain and barriers to love and I allow my heart to heal.'*

✧ Visualise a stream of darkness leaving your heart and flowing away. A bright light touches the stream and turns it to molten gold. All your pain and heartache is dissolved into strength and wisdom.

✧ See the door wide open and feel the love that is now flowing in. Allow yourself to be caressed and filled with this love. It goes deeper and deeper into your heart, finding every last trace of hurt and sense of loss and dissolving it — love heals everything it touches.

Bless you.

THE HEART OPENING SYMBOL

This symbol will assist your commitment and determination to open your heart. It acts as a communication between you and your heart, holding your intention to open yourself to love. Draw it three times over your heart centre, then place your hand on your heart centre and again visualise the door opening.

Heart opening symbol

Allocate a few minutes every day to use the symbol and visualisation.

HEALING YOUR HEART

Whenever you have been hurt by the loss of love your emotional heart will be wounded and scarred. These scars act as barriers to love so you will need to heal these old wounds to enable your heart to open fully to give and receive love. It is, therefore, important to focus on anything and everything that can help you to heal your heart. Write down your pain and grief. Forgive anyone who has left you and broken your heart and move on. Understand that you need love in any form: from God, from creation, through nature, through friends, through work you love to do, through hobbies and pastimes that make you smile. Find activities and people who make you laugh and lift your spirits. The following chapters are full of help for your healing. Now move on to the next step – your intention to dissolve the separation.

INTEND TO END THE SEPARATION

The driving force of change is intention, followed by will and determination. Nothing can start to change within you and for you unless you give your permission. You have free will so you can choose to change. As we have seen, free will is the gift you bring to Earth to help you manage your life here. Anything you decided before you came can be modified through your ability to choose. One day you will become enlightened and will leave the cycle of life and death and return home. In the meantime just follow your heart and what feels good for you. At this moment you need to bring your free will into play and make the choice to reconnect. Are you now ready to realign and reconnect to your Higher Self and accept your divinity?

Are you? If you are, then say so out loud! This will re-inforce your commitment, which is essential for the success of the process we are about to set in motion. Say the following intention out loud, using your own words if you wish:

'I intend to integrate the energies of my monad, my Higher Self, my I AM self, my divine presence, with my heart and soul.'

Say it three times in total. You may feel a frisson running through your body, or another sensation of some kind. This will be your soul's reaction to what it has waited for so long. Write down the words of your intention and put them in a special place. Make this a daily mantra, a confirmation of your intention and a great lead-up to the actual visualisation and integration process.

Well done! You are well on the way now to reconnecting with that most amazing aspect of your true self. In the next chapter I will lead you through the process of connection and integration that will bring your two spiritual aspects together and release the powerful forces of divine love that have been out of reach during the time of your separation.

THREE

Reconnecting and Integration

'I had a feeling of becoming whole and coming home –
I feel stronger and at peace'
Jen Khoo, the first person I took through the process of
integration

In this chapter I will guide you through a meditation and
visualisation that will re-establish the connection to your
divine self, your Higher Self. Of course, the connection is
always there, it's just that we forget about it. In our minds
we see ourselves as mere mortals going through the challenges and ups and downs of life. We go through life hoping
to meet love, hoping to find fulfilment in our work, hoping
to have families, hoping we won't get ill or be a burden to
our loved ones. We live in a material world where the focus
is on where we live, what we eat, success in terms of money
and status. Little time seems to be available for our spiritual
resuscitation and fulfilment. We feel limited in what we can
do and confined by what we allow ourselves to do. Many
of us find ourselves working and living in the closed and

restricted world of the physical and react exclusively to emotions and thoughts, influences and attitudes, that have nothing to do with the 'real' world or the 'real' people that we are. We will continue to flounder around trying to fix and patch up our society and our own lives until we see our lives as a joint venture with spirit and respect and confirm our spirituality as a matter of course.

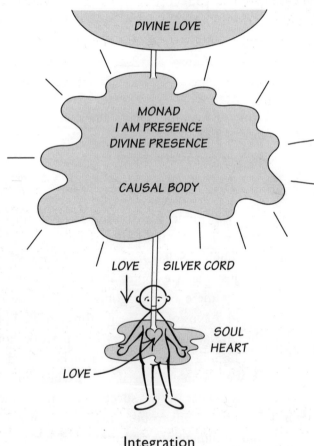

Integration

Now we come to the process that I have taken many people through over the last few years. Through this we will lift the energy of your soul and bring it to the frequency and purity of love that matches the energy of your monad. Remember, your Higher Self has not suffered the wounding and negative experiences that your soul has been through. It has always stayed as it was created – holding the light; holding the frequency of unconditional love; holding the purpose which God gave it at your conception as an individual divine spark; holding the ability to create whatever it needs to fulfil its purpose. When you integrate this energy with the rest of you – mind, emotions, character, ego, physical form and soul – then this pure energy will flow through you and everything you do.

The integration ceremony

Take about an hour for this meditation and make it a full ceremony. You will need time to allow the energies to be realigned and flow through you. You can perform the visualisation as many times as you wish. You may find it beneficial to have a friend with you who can lead you through it and say the words out loud or you can read it to yourself and imagine that I am saying these words to you. I have also recorded it on a CD (see the Resources section at the end of the book). When you have finished the visualisation, sit or lie quietly for at least half an hour to allow the energies to continue to work for you.

✧ Find a very quiet space. Clear the room with a smudge stick or other cleansing process. Make it special by burning your favourite aromatherapy oils or incense. If you have a favourite crystal, bring it to the room with you.

✧ Bless the room by asking your angels, spirit guides or your favourite spiritual or religious leader to fill the room with love and be with you during the ceremony. If you do Reiki or other healing, bring in healing energies to fill the room.

✧ Place a candle and fresh flowers near your seat.

✧ As you read this, I am helping you with your integration and I am connecting to you through your heart centre. Our hearts will touch and a flow of divine love will be channelled through me to you to lift the energy of your soul to your divine self. You simply have to allow it to flow in as you read:

We call in your spirit guides and angels and my spirit guides to assist with this integration. We ask all those in spirit who love you and wish to assist you to come through with their loving intention now.

I place you in a pink ball of light filled with love. I place around the room you are in a blue cordon of light that only love can enter. You are now in a beautiful sacred and loving place for your integration.

✧ Please say out loud again, '*I am ready for my soul integration.*' Bless you.

See the door of your heart opening to receive love. My heart touches your heart and divine love flows through the open door of your heart, filling your heart. It fills your heart to overflowing and keeps coming. More love and more love fills you and your heart.

More love comes and moves through every cell of your body. Every cell has a heart centre that is yearning for love. The love continues to flow and fills your soul with love. Your soul is filled to overflowing with love and it fills every wound in your soul. Your soul is healed with love.

As your soul is filled with love it now rises up your silver cord to meet the energy of your monad. You are now reunited with your Higher Self and become as one.

✧ Raise your hand above your head and bring it down, encouraging the flow of loving energy to fill your entire being. Do this a number of times. As you do this, say 'My heart and soul are fully integrated with my Divine Presence.' Repeat three times.

✧ Breathe deeply and allow the energies to flow. You are blessed.

✧ Now rest for at least half an hour to allow the energies to settle and for the integration to anchor. You have merged and integrated with different energies – the energy of your soul and the energy of your Higher Self. They need time to settle together.

OUTCOMES

Your integration may affect you in a number of ways. I will go through some of these with you now.

PEACE AND RELIEF

Immediately you may feel a sense of peace, and experience the feeling that you have come home. These feelings are the outcome of the merging together of higher and lower selves. It may have been a long, long time since you were fully flowing as a spiritual being, for you may have been separated for many lifetimes. You may feel a great sense of relief, as though a burden and tension has left you. Remember, your soul has wanted this love for eons. It will have been completely filled with love, both from the divine energies you received through your heart and the energies of pure love and wisdom from your divine self.

LIGHT-HEADEDNESS

The high vibrations of love may make you feel a little spacey and light-headed. If you feel disorientated, just take a little longer before you get back into your daily routine. You can ground yourself by eating cheese – yes, truly! You can also ground yourself with crystals like tourmaline, red jasper and obsidian. Or close your eyes and visualise yourself as a great tree and see your roots growing down deep into the earth. Allow yourself to be connected to the earth energies. It is helpful to take a walk outside on grass, preferably barefoot. But don't drive if you are very light-headed.

INTENSE EMOTION

You may feel weepy and emotional. This will be a reaction to the relief that you feel at letting go negativity and experiencing the in-surge of love, and to the healing that this in itself creates. I always cry when I feel and sense great love, and in this situation you are feeling both a surge of love through your heart and the love of your own divine self.

The very understanding that you have been feeling abandoned, alone or unloved through no fault of your own is another trigger that can make you feel emotional. Let the tears flow whenever they start coming as these are a sign that you are letting go of old emotions. You might find you experience a roller-coaster of emotions – feeling elated one minute, then sad, then joyous, and so on. This is part of the healing process and is quite normal. After a while you will settle down.

CONFIDENCE

One day you may feel like Superwoman/man – as if you can take on the world and everything is possible. The next you will feel yourself incapable of boiling an egg. This is a typical reaction following any process of healing. You are making the connection then losing it. While you are in this back and forth state before you achieve total connection, you will have moments when you feel unsure of yourself, followed by times when you feel brilliant. Be aware that this is a process you are going through and allow it to take its course.

Any major shift is an opportunity to re-evaluate your self-esteem and to start to respect yourself more. Taking you closer to the peaceful state where – in a loving way, of course – you don't really bother too much about other people's perspective of you. If people are dismissive of you, argu-mentative, judgemental or just provocative, remember it's probably their issues that are coming up – your self-confidence may be pushing their buttons! Keep your cool and they will back off. You will generally find that once you become more confident you will attract other people who are peaceful and self-assured, for like will attract like.

INTUITION

When you make your integration you become connected to your causal body, the information database of everything you have every learnt or experienced. This can improve your intuitive powers so that you find yourself 'feeling' what you want to do rather than logically deducing the best options. It will help you to know what is best for you rather than making decisions based on what you 'think' is the right choice.

For example, one of my students, Betty, always struggled with what she wanted in life. She dithered over every decision, no matter how big or small. She asked me for clarity, which of course is not an easy gift to give someone else. She also wanted answers. I told her that she was the one to make the choices, but suggested I help her to reconnect and integrate to her Higher Self. Then she would be more in touch with her true self, which should help her indecisiveness. After she went through the process and the energies had settled, she rang me to say everything was working well in her life. She had a new job, she had enrolled on a new course and she felt sure of herself in a way she had never done before.

MANIFESTING

As your connection becomes stronger, so does your ability to create and manifest what you want. This is because you become at one with the energy of creation – the true essence of who you are. This, of course, can work for or against you! If you are feeling negative and pessimistic, then you will draw towards you negative situations and people. Some days you will seem to be in confrontation with awkward and angry people – taxis disappear, shop assistants are difficult, your children play up, the fridge breaks and you feel unloved by all and sundry. Other days you will be more positive, and this will set off a positive cycle around you.

SICKNESS

I will be taking you through a range of ways to heal in the following chapters; ways to release the saboteurs that prevent you from connecting permanently and completely. Integration is a form of healing process and the outcome can often be sickness, caused by your soul and heart releasing their wounds and pain through your physical body. As the pain cannot be sent from your soul upwards, it has to be dispersed through your physical body, which gets the worst of it. But remember, it will be the dispersing of old energies; old wounds healing; past trauma and guilt being released. So it's a positive process, even if you feel pretty lousy while it goes on. Old tears may be released as a cold, blocks to your throat energy centre may be caused by unexpressed feelings and may manifest as sore throats, while heart pain can come out as chest infections. Just take care of yourself, allow yourself time off to rest and recuperate. Have a hot toddy and take a hot water bottle to bed. Be gentle and kind to yourself and don't push on with your normal routine.

All the above symptoms come as a result of healing – which is releasing old negative imprints and blocks and allowing yourself to be loved, to be connected and to be free. As with the integration, any of the healing processes I take you through in this book can trigger reactions. But know that these are all reactions that lead you to a better place, a better feeling and a happier inner state. Try not to over-analyse what is happening if you go through emotional or physical reactions, just go with the flow of the process. Afterwards, when you feel calmer and stronger, look back and see if you can grasp what was going on. Then you can understand the negativity that you were releasing; the challenging situations you had drawn into your life; why you attracted a certain person or a certain situation; what you gained from a confrontation; what you learned about yourself.

HOW TO STAY CONNECTED AND INTEGRATED

All the above reactions are a result of making a connection that comes and goes. It's quite normal to have them and it's a rare person who makes a full and permanent integration in one attempt. Usually our minds step in with old negative attitudes and thought processes, while the challenges of those around us often make us doubt ourselves. You may well fall back into old patterns and habits. So I am now going to go through a number of ways in which you can help yourself to hold the intention of your connection and keep the energy of your spiritual aspect flowing through you.

HOLD THE INTENTION

Keep the goal of becoming fully in touch with your divine aspect high on your list of priorities. Make it one of your life goals, along with finding love, a good job, a home, children and so on. If you pray, then ask God for help with this. If you prefer, you can create affirmations to say out loud every morning as part of your daily routine. Here are a few ideas you can use or interpret with your own words:

I am fully connected and integrated with my divine presence.
I claim my higher powers.
I am in touch with my true self.
I am at one with my Higher Self.

ALLOW TIME

You will need time on two counts. First, it will take time to heal all your saboteurs, the blocks that prevent your full integration. Second, you will need to take time for yourself to allow the process to activate.

✧ Take time for yourself. Have me time. Visit a spa, take up a hobby, join a slimming group, book a holiday, watch your favourite DVDs, take walks or choose a form of exercise that suits you.

✧ Take time to meditate, to sit quietly and focus on some aspect of yourself that needs loving. There are a number of meditation exercises throughout this book which you can use. Also I have recorded CDs of healing meditations that allow you to focus on aspects of yourself that you know need love and healing (see Resources at the end of the book).

✧ Take time for contemplation – just sit and do nothing. Wow, that will be a first! Simply do nothing – no meditation, no actual doing of any kind. Let your thoughts go where they will. If they go to the negative cupboard, close the door and gently lead them to the positives in your life.

✧ Take time for gratitude. Think of all the good things in your life – write a list. Keep focusing on all the lucky breaks you've had, the great people that have helped you, the friends who support and love you, the family, your pets, etc. Gratitude is a wonderful way to lift your spirits and it opens the channel to your spiritual aspect.

BEWARE DISTRACTIONS

You will face challenges in your daily life that may take you away from your acceptance of being divine and claiming your powers. Watch out for these and take action when you find you are falling into their traps.

Trying to please other people

If you allow other people's needs and happiness to dominate everything you do, you are in danger of submerging your own desires and feelings. It's fine to take the needs of family, friends and colleagues into account but, if they are the total focus of your life, then you will be living your life from the wrong perspective. You will start to ignore your intuition and sense of what is right and supportive for you.

This doesn't mean you have to be selfish and uncaring or totally self-centred. But ensure you keep a balance between your life needs and those of others. Speak up and say what you feel – lovingly but firmly. Keep your boundaries – say no sometimes if someone wants to take time that you had allocated for your own rest and recuperation. Beware the tendency towards martyrdom and self-sabotage – these are not spiritually evolved traits. They are destructive and negative and they make other people feel guilty, or can bring out the bully in them. There is never a need to subjugate yourself to another person. So keep an eye on this balance between the needs of yourself and others.

Lack of self-love

This is sometimes related to the previous point. You may well find that you put other people first because you do not value yourself. Remind yourself that you are equal to anyone else and need to be high on the list for loving. In fact there is an argument for you being number one, on the basis that if you love yourself and respect yourself fully then you will automatically spread that love to others. While you are struggling with judgement of yourself you will tend to judge others.

There will be reasons why you have shut down on yourself, why you have a low opinion and respect of yourself. Work on finding the root cause of this problem and look for ways to heal it. In the following chapters we will be focusing on the potential causes of low self-esteem, so keep yourself open to the ones that may lie at the root of your problem. In the meantime hold the intention of putting yourself higher up the list and judging yourself less harshly. Self-judgement is a serious impediment to considering yourself divine and accessing your higher powers.

Fear

All fears have to be released at some stage as they are blocks to your enlightenment. Keep yourself open to finding the root cause behind any unnatural fear or anxiety – again, you may find the cause within this book – and keep hold of your intention to heal it. Many people go through their lives pronouncing their fear of this or that without any conscious intention to release these fears. They will have to go through lifetime after lifetime facing these fears if they do not let them go. Fear is a fundamental symptom of an old wound from a past experience and is a powerful clue that can lead you to a deep problem that needs resolving. Don't accept fear as a way of life.

WORKING WITH YOUR PERSONALITY AND CHARACTER

To keep your connection strong you will need to be honest about yourself and to spend time consciously recognising who you are and accepting yourself. If you are always being critical of yourself, you are creating a negative charge that acts as a barrier to your higher self. To start with it's important to get to know yourself well. This will bring understanding and acceptance and will be beneficial in strengthening your connection. Self-acceptance is a form of self-love and your aim is to love yourself fully and unconditionally, to allow yourself to raise your energy to the monadic state of love.

Your personality is the most obvious expression of who you are to the outside world – it affects your relationships with those around you and the world as a whole. It will affect the ease with which you interface to other people and how you see yourself. Your character is made up of a composition of your genetic inheritance, of the traits and attitudes inherited from your parents and forbears, of your life experiences, the good and bad experiences you have had from early childhood onwards, and the effects of your birth date and time – the effects of the planets at the time you were born. Instead of only being critical of yourself, let's focus on which of these various influences can be consciously changed and which you just have to learn to live with, bearing in mind that you will have chosen your major traits to suit the work and challenges you plan to tackle in this lifetime.

Plenty of emphasis has been put on the effects of DNA, the biological inheritance that was formed by your ancestors' development. It's normally accepted that we cannot change this. However, I have had some surprising results in my healing sessions when I have worked on the stream of energy that flows to us from our parents and beyond. In Chapter 4 I share ways in which you can heal physical, mental and emotional aspects of yourself that you feel are attributable to your family history.

As you work on discovering what makes you tick, you will come across attitudes and programming that have been passed to you by your parents and close relatives – in fact by anyone who has had an influence on you in the past, especially in childhood, when you were impressionable and liable to copy those you admired or loved. Always keep an open mind about the ability to change anything that you have decided you want to change about yourself, but try not to fall into the trap of blaming those who may have encouraged such aspects of your character. In other words, avoid telling the world that you have a temper that came from your father with the attitude that it's a given and in no way can it be changed. You can learn to manage your anger, whether it came from your father or whether it is caused by deep frustration with situations in your life. Don't let your discovery of yourself turn into a cause for blame, of others or yourself.

Understanding your character

Here is an exercise to help you understand your own personality and character. Ask yourself the question, What am I like? Do this without self-criticism, for that's going to get you nowhere except feeling bad about yourself – a definite step backwards! Put a tick against any of the following characteristics that you think describe you, and add anything I haven't mentioned:

Personality trait	All the time	Occasionally	Never
Self-critical	☐	☐	☐
Controlling of self or others	☐	☐	☐
Perfectionist	☐	☐	☐
Reserved, quiet or secretive	☐	☐	☐
Driven, pushing towards goals	☐	☐	☐
Hyperactive and on the go all the time	☐	☐	☐
Laid back and relaxed	☐	☐	☐
Quick to anger and irritable	☐	☐	☐
Loving and compassionate	☐	☐	☐
Passionate about issues and people	☐	☐	☐
Forward thinking and a planner	☐	☐	☐
Optimistic, expect the best	☐	☐	☐
Pessimistic, fear the worst	☐	☐	☐
Think of others before yourself, find it difficult to refuse anyone	☐	☐	☐
Self-aware and self-focused (this does not mean selfish!)	☐	☐	☐
Anxious and fearful of the unknown	☐	☐	☐
Happy and bright as a natural state	☐	☐	☐
Depressive and downcast more often than upbeat	☐	☐	☐
A chatterbox who finds it easy to talk to strangers	☐	☐	☐
Find it difficult to relate to new people, dislike crowds	☐	☐	☐

Personality trait	All the time	Occasionally	Never
Liable to mood swings, up and down temperamentally	☐	☐	☐
A daydreamer, ungrounded	☐	☐	☐
Practical, a 'make it happen' person	☐	☐	☐
Excitable	☐	☐	☐
Phlegmatic, take it as it comes	☐	☐	☐
Outgoing and extrovert	☐	☐	☐

Spend some time thinking about yourself. How do you think you project yourself to others? Get friends and work colleagues to tick the boxes and compare. Make an intention to know yourself and identify any characteristics that you feel you are lacking and which you would like to enhance, for example courage, flexibility, patience or expressiveness. As part of this exercise, take a look at your characteristics and see which of them are purely adopted from your parents. How many are habitual? Could you change any of your characteristics? Do you want to change, or are you completely happy with the way you are? That is perfectly OK too.

If you have characteristics and traits that are difficult to live with, you will create reactions from those around you. This will affect your emotional state. For example, if you are prickly and withdrawn, finding it difficult to relate to new people or lacking trust, then you may find that people avoid you, or react in a curt, offhand or angry manner. You may find this upsetting, and it can encourage you to mistrust others and be even more withdrawn yourself.

Realise that people can only react to the energy and the face you present — an open and happy face will always get a better response than an impatient or off-putting manner. If you want people to accept you and love you, then your goal will be to develop uplifting, positive traits, letting go those driven by anger, lassitude, impatience, self-dislike, intolerance, etc. Your overall goal is to feel better inside and out, mentally, physically and emotionally. If you feel better you will find you respond to the world and those around you more congenially.

PLAY TO YOUR STRENGTHS

When your confidence goes walkabout and you feel depressed about your achievements, then focus on all the things that you are good at. Write a list of everything you have ever achieved in order to remind you of what you can do. Understand that you have the skills and abilities that you need for this lifetime. Not everyone needs to be a great painter, a brilliant scholar, a successful salesman or a speaker, teacher or writer. We all have the skill sets that we need. So look at what you can do. Do you listen well? Can you make people feel good about themselves? Do you exude kindness and care? Do you bring balance to a group of people? Do you inspire others? Do you care for animals? Do you make people laugh and see the funny side of situations? Are you strong in a crisis? And so on.

TAKE ANY OPPORTUNITY TO HEAL

Let it be your intention to heal and bring yourself into total balance. Healing is the releasing of a negative charge that is held in some aspect of your mind, emotions or soul that has been caused by a past experience. There are many ways you can find healing:

✧ Fixing a physical problem using modern surgical options.

✧ Self-healing through time, love and care of yourself.

✧ Using alternative therapies such as acupuncture, reflex-ology, cranial work, Emotional Freedom Technique (EFT) and so on.

✧ Visiting healers who can help you identify the cause of your problem and assist you to release it and bring your energy vibrations up, lifting your spirits and opening you to the possibility of full happiness and contentment.

✧ Reading books, attending workshops and seminars that help you understand yourself and the way you work.

Don't accept limitations. Keep on trying to find ways to clear the problems that trouble you.

In the following chapters I will guide you through a number of causes for the blocks that may hold you in a state of separation. I will show you the wounds and imprints (the memories of past trauma embedded in your subconscious) that may be the underlying cause of your current problems and how to resolve them. I will start by looking at what makes you tick – the different aspects that make up your whole – and how these can fall out of harmony with each other and how you can bring them back together. In other words, I will help you bring yourself into balance. This is a great opportunity to heal!

Remember who you are - the essence of divine love.

FOUR

Creating Balance and Harmony

If the children are fighting amongst themselves they are not taking notice of the teacher. It's essential for you to bring your holistic self of mind, emotions, spirit, ego and body into harmony if you want to be connected to the wisdom of your Divine Self.

Now you have set a goal and know where you are going, you need to work through everything that has the potential to obstruct your connection: all the wounds, scars and bad memories of the past, the guilt, fears and anxieties that these bring up, and the disharmony that may be taking you off course. In this chapter I will focus on helping you to harmonise the different components that make up the whole that is you. You will learn to allow these different facets of yourself to work together in harmony; to acknowledge consciously that you are more than just physical form; to respect everything that makes you a unique and special being; to encourage each component to be of equal importance and to come into complete holistic balance.

THE FACETS THAT MAKE UP THE WHOLE YOU

Let's first see what these different facets are that make up your entire being – what we often refer to as the holistic self. Then I will take you through the ways that they may be suffering from your separation from your Higher Self and show you how you can heal them. I will be referring to these as bodies in order to show that they are in fact full aspects, distinct bodies that have different roles to make up the whole that is you. There is a constant interlinking and exchange of understanding and energies between them and the thoughts and senses that affect their relationship with each other.

These are your holistic facets:

✧ mental body
✧ emotional body
✧ spiritual body
✧ ego
✧ physical body

You might like to see them as separate bodies – maybe the illustration overleaf will help you to visualise their links to each other.

OUR COMPONENT PARTS

Let's look at these facets in more detail, see how they affect each other and how we can heal them. These components, aspects of our holistic make-up, remind me of the Mr Men characters for children. Some are wayward and some have a tendency to be aggressive, and there is one they all beat up – just like children in a playground.

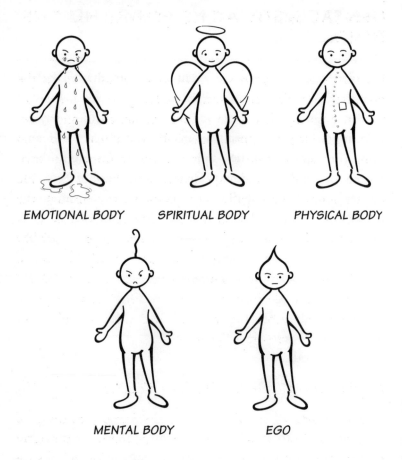

EMOTIONAL BODY   SPIRITUAL BODY   PHYSICAL BODY

MENTAL BODY   EGO

Our holistic bodies

Once we have seen their roles, how they affect each other and found ways to heal each component, then we can work on bringing them into harmony with each other in order to ensure that our little facet figures stop beating each other up!

We'll start by looking at the role of the mental body.

MENTAL BODY – THE POWER OF THE MIND

He (sorry, but I always see this part of us as a he!) is the organiser and planner of our lives. He plays an important role in ensuring that there is some organisation and order in your life. He passes through inspirations that may be sourced from your spirit, from the spirit world or from your own source of wisdom and experience, your Higher Self. He creates positive or negative charges of energy through the rest of your system and can have a huge influence on how uplifted or depressed you are. He can manage your life for you or create chaos. He can be calm and peaceful or out of control and manic. He has huge power which can work for or against you. Healing the mind and holding it in peace will be an enormous step forward to clearing the obstacles between you and your Higher Self.

MIND WORKING WITH CREATION

The state of your mind is vital to the healthy running of your physical body and is the holder of the most powerful aspect of thought – intention, which can make changes on every level of your being. When an intention is strong and held firmly in focus, it creates a bubble of thought – a positive thought pattern – and the energy of that thought sends out a message to the world. This message sets in action a spiritual law – the law of attraction. The energy vibration and pattern that is represented in the thought form attracts into form and matter the desire or need that you are holding in your thought. In other words, whatever you wish for you get. We call this manifesting; creating what you want in your life.

But the mind has to be focused for this to work well, and your other facets have to be in line and of the same accord. Your emotions must be happy with this new desire – it's not going to work if, for example, the thought of a new job brings up from your emotional body fears of responsibility and anxiety about change. So you need to heal a mind that is troubled and unfocused in order to manifest and you need to heal your emotional body so that it doesn't sabotage your intentions. Remember that the law of attraction always works, so if you are sending out fearful visualisations and negative thoughts you will be attracting the same negative situations that you are so anxious about.

Check your words and thoughts and try to keep them as positive as possible.

BELIEFS AND A CLOSED MIND

The mind has the tendency to be driven by beliefs, some of which may be outdated and inherited from family, culture or religion. In extreme cases the mind can be so programmed that individual thought – the independence of the mental body – no longer exists. For example, you may have been brought up to believe that you will go to hell if you don't go to church on Sunday. If you then go against this belief, there is the danger that as you are dying you will be holding this belief in your mind and you will die fearfully, expecting hell to be waiting for you.

Children will often be indoctrinated by their parents with their beliefs, so you may have to reprogramme yourself and let go beliefs that don't work for you as you reach adulthood. For example, if you have been told you are useless and stupid, you will believe this until you can prove to yourself otherwise. I am sure that we do not truly trust a belief in adulthood unless we experience it for ourselves. Once you have started to achieve and find success in the world then you can start to believe you are of value and capable.

The danger is that, despite achieving success, you may still fail to accept yourself and persistently hold on to the old belief that your parents instilled into you. Healing and therapies can help you break down old beliefs and programming. Emotional Freedom Technique (EFT) and Neuro-linguistic Programming (NLP) are both therapies that help you de-programme old patterns and allow you to accept new concepts and perceptions of yourself and life. Details and contacts for these therapies can be found in the Resources section.

Whatever course you take, it's important to have an open mind. Many people have come to me for treatment sceptical and unsure but open to the possibility that I can help them. These people will always gain something from the experience, for they are open to try. Having an open mind is hugely important when it comes to healing Mr Mental.

Experience can change beliefs when your mind is open;
your mind can heal you when it is receptive to the
needs of the rest of your being.

NEGATIVE THOUGHTS

A mind that continually feeds negative thoughts towards yourself or others will be most destructive and a major cause of separation. Negative thoughts are the result of worry, anxiety, fear, anger, guilt, low self-esteem and criticism of self and others. Usually there will be a deeper wound beneath that causes this mindset, so if you tend to see the dark side and expect the worst from everything and everybody, don't worry. We will be looking into healing the wounds that may be creating these attitudes later on. In the meantime we will look at ways in which you can reprogramme yourself to think positively and find why you might be holding this pattern.

A closed mind, a negative mind or a controlling mind can be a serious cause of separation.

The traits of a negative mind include the following:

✧ It is overpowering, controlling. It knows best and holds you on a course of action due to old programmed belief systems.

✧ It is unfocused and confused, darting from one idea or thought to another and unable to stay with one subject or goal long enough to see it through.

✧ It elbows out the heart and soul (Mr Spiritual) and takes charge of decisions, choosing logic rather than heartfelt feelings.

✧ It dismisses messages from spirit as 'imagination' and there-fore not valid. In fact your imagination is your channel from spirit, in the form of angels and spiritual guides, your Higher Self and your soul, and needs to be acknowl-edged for a balanced view.

✧ It overrides the needs of the body with 'must do' inten-tions, driving it on through the belief that action is more important than rest and following other old programming such as 'I promised, so I will do it no matter what the cost to myself'. This causes burnout and exhaustion.

✧ It uses negative thinking that attacks ego and emotions, such as 'I am no good because I have been told so', shattering confidence and creating anxiety that churns up negative emotions.

✧ It allows negative thoughts of desires and needs to dominate, such as 'I must have' – as experienced in addictions.

✧ It is closed to new thoughts, beliefs and experiences. This is the mindset of many followers of faiths and religions, disallowing any benefits that new thoughts and ideas might have. In extreme cases this can lead to a lack of spiritual tolerance and dismissal of the benefits of modern medicine and science.

✧ It returns to the past and relives past trauma, loss, sadness, actions of self and others and feeds the emotional body with guilt, bitterness, anger and hate.

✧ It judges yourself and others, drawing down your spirits and causing your emotions to feel lack of love or even hatred of yourself – a sure way to move out of alignment and connection with the vibrations of love of your Higher Self.

ACTIVELY CREATING POSITIVE ENERGY THOUGHTS

To counter our negative tendencies, here are a few ways you can refocus your mind to create uplifting or positive thought streams:

Gratitude

This is first on the list as it creates an immediate charge of positive energy and uplifts spiritually and emotionally. Think of everything that you can be thankful for. If you feel in the mood, make a list and pin it on your wall or stick it on the fridge. My brother-in-law recently had a heart attack that thankfully was resolved by major restorative heart surgery. He and my sister are so thankful that he has survived, they say, that nothing can get to them now, nothing will get them down. They are just so grateful for life. This is a major key to turning your negativity around.

Be in the present

The past can be full of elephant traps, making you relive traumatic and distressing experiences. The future is unknown and out of your control. If you insist on focusing on the future, you will be fighting battles and facing problems that may never happen. The present is usually a far safer place to be. Eckhart Tolle has written a great book, *The Power of Now*, about how he turned his life around just by focusing on the present.

Positive intentions

Saying out loud your positive intentions and affirming how you want to be can be very powerful. Whenever I want to change something in my life I declare that it's already happening, for example 'I attract the finances I need'. Use declarations like this to counteract any pessimistic tendencies that you may have.

There are many other ways to 'turn positive'. Why don't you think of a few that would work for you? Remember that your negative words, thoughts and attitudes affect your physical body, your emotions and your spirit, and that these are YOU! They also affect all those around you. If you give out a negative energy flow, you will attract negativity from everyone else. If you are in a positive frame of mind then you will attract uplifting and positive people and situations. That's how it works.

LACK OF FOCUS – A BUTTERFLY MIND

This most powerful of all the facets of our holistic self (apart from the spiritual body) is the one that Buddha gave a great deal of attention to in his belief system. One reason may be that it's within our conscious power to affect its workings. His teachings show that by calming and controlling the mind we have access to the higher spiritual aspect of self. In other words, if we control the mind, cleanse it of negative thoughts like worry and fear, then we can open ourselves to our true spirituality – our divine self, our Higher Self. Thoughts that fly from subject to subject send your energy outwards and by the end of the day you can feel depleted and tired. On some days you may be thinking of your mother's birthday present one minute, what to cook for dinner the next, how to approach the boss for a pay rise after that, and then what you are going to say to your neighbour about their noisy teenagers. You will definitely be exhausted by the evening – if you get there without nodding off! On other days, when you are able to spend all your time focused on something you enjoy, you will find yourself uplifted and energised. So you need to control a butterfly mind that wanders off to unsolved problems, to magnify situations by constantly chewing them over, to avoid the most important issues and flit to the minu-tiae, to relive the traumas of the past over and over again, and bring it into balance and harmony with the rest of your being.

Calming a turbulent mind

Here is a breathing technique that will also help slow down and calm your emotions and physical body. While you focus on your breathing, you will not be worrying or becoming stressed about the things that are making you anxious. This is a good exercise to do in the morning before you start your daily round, around lunchtime and to clear your mind before bedtime.

✧ Sit comfortably in a quiet place, turn off phones and the TV.

✧ Take a slow breath in through your right nostril. Now breathe out, letting the breath flow through your left nostril.

✧ When you take your next breath do the same, but relax your stomach as you breathe in. The calming breath will go deep into the place where you keep your fear – your solar plexus.

✧ Slowly release this breath. Let your shoulders drop and pull your stomach in to get rid of every last drop of breath.

✧ Continue these last two steps for five minutes.

The mind as an energy zapper or uplifter of spirits

Every thought you have is a shaft of energy. If you are creating positive thoughts your spiritual body will get the benefit as your spirits become uplifted, your emotional body will feel good, your physical body will benefit by the uplifted energy stream and can even let go of certain illnesses that arise from low energy.

It's essential that you find time to calm your mind, focus

and work towards programming your thoughts into a positive direction.

Attachments to the past

Finally we look at one of the most destructive tendencies of a wayward mind: the need to keep revisiting negative situations from the past. This tendency to float back to the past and relive pain, suffering, grief and injustice can set up a number of negative emotions. When you go back you are reliving the negative experience again and again. You will bring forth negative emotions such as anger, sadness, self-pity and blame. As the illustration shows, you may find you go back so often to wallow in the past that you create a mudpatch. Before long you will find yourself stuck there!

Don't get stuck in the mud!

Letting go of the past

The following exercise will assist you in letting go of your attachment to the past, something that will be greatly beneficial in your control of the mind.

✧ Close your eyes, drop your shoulders and relax.

✧ Say out loud your intention to let go of the past: '*I am setting myself free from the past. I let go all my attachments and interest in people and situations that have hurt me in the past.*'

✧ Allow yourself to go back one last time to the person or experience that you want to release. See it and feel it. Decide whether you want it and all its pain to remain in your life. Do you want it? Do you need it? Does it make you feel good and strong?

✧ Say your last goodbye to the person or situation. Visualise yourself turning and walking away for the last time.

✧ Make a vow never to return – NEVER GO BACK. '*I have no reason to go back – I will never return to that again.*'

✧ Now focus on one of your blessings. It could be a person who loves you, a skill or gift you have, a garden, a home – whatever you consider a blessing. Spend a few moments thinking about this now.

✧ If you find at any time that your mind slips backwards, deliberately turn it around and make it focus on your blessing. Use your blessing like a lucky mascot and keep it close to your thoughts at all times.

As our thoughts and emotions become positive and
uplifted, so we come closer to the state of love. This
brings us ever nearer to the pure love of our Higher Self.

THE EMOTIONAL BODY – HOW YOU FEEL

Our emotional body probably causes us some of our worst pain, and this happens from an early age. Children experience emotional trauma but, of course, if they live in a loving environment they can express it and release it quickly and effectively. One quick burst of crying and most often it's all gone. As we get older, though, we feel we have to suppress our emotions – and that's when the real problems begin.

Emotional pain is hard to cope with because it cannot be seen or measured. You don't know what other people feel and you don't know if how you feel is normal, abnormal, extreme or just OK. You usually only realise how 'bad' you have been feeling when something or someone helps you to feel better. I know that was certainly true for me. Throughout my life I held a sense of anxiety so subtle that I couldn't explain it to anyone. Often it would flare up into full-blown anxiety and then it would be easier to quantify. I would have a focus for my fear and I could identify the cause: 'I'm frightened of horses'; 'France upsets me and makes me ill'; 'I don't like crowds'; 'aggression on TV disturbs me'; 'any confrontation upsets me'.

Once I started to heal my inner wounds and let go of old emotions, I found that I felt good inside. I felt calm most of the time and those things that used to send me into a tizzy were no longer a problem. In fact I love horses now and have a holiday home in France! In my previous state it was as if there was a constant background noise of anxiety.

I must say it's wonderful now not to have it, not to have butterflies in my stomach or the indigestion and digestive disorders that went with it.

So our emotions can easily disturb our physical state of wellbeing and cause a number of ailments and illnesses. Here are just a few of the more obvious problems our physical body creates from our emotional distress. A number of our illnesses have roots in fear, anger and lack of self-love and respect. For example arthritis is associated with self-criticism, anger can trigger liver problems and raise your blood pressure, and bitterness can upset the gall bladder.

STRESS

Stress will always pull you away from your spiritual intentions. It encourages negative feelings and thoughts, and can even affect your physical state. These are all distractions from your spiritual connection.

Stress is considered a modern-day illness – although I am sure I would have been extremely stressed if I had been a worker in a Victorian factory, married to a drunk and trying to feed eleven children! I think that it's probably been around as long as we have had families and responsibilities.

In order to deal with stress you first need to acknowledge that you are suffering from it. Stress can go unnoticed when you are enjoying your life and having fun, and it may be that you only become aware of the condition when one of the illnesses or ailments listed below kicks in. I must say that if I had been asked whether I felt stress when I was in my thirties, I would have said 'No, but I am excited about my work'! My husband, Tony, always declared he never suffered from stress; he enjoyed his high-powered work but no, he never felt the pressure on his body or emotions. One day he had to have a medical checkup right after a lively board meeting and he was shocked to find that his normally low blood pressure had shot up. He then realised that this probably happened at all the highly charged meetings he attended without him being aware of it.

Stress is an anxiety which is created by the pressure of our daily lives: of expectations, lack of time, intention to please self and others, financial demands, etc. It can cause a number of symptoms and ailments, including lack of energy and exhaustion. If you have been hyperactive during the day, you will either go on to a state of exhaustion in the evening with your body unable to move from the couch, or you will feel so stimulated you end up spending a sleepless night, worrying till dawn – giving a hard time to Mr Mental!

These emotional pressures can create a number of ailments. Here are just some of the symptoms that stress can trigger:

✧ Headache, especially migraine.

✧ Indigestion – stress activates the production of stomach acid.

✧ Stomach ulcers – like indigestion, these are caused by stomach acid, but are more serious as the stomach wall is affected.

✧ High blood pressure – our heart goes into overdrive when it picks up the fight or flight messages of fear.

✧ Heart disease – stress increases the level of cholesterol in the blood, blocking the veins and arteries that feed the heart.

✧ Insomnia.

When your emotions take over you lose inner peace and you lose touch with your spiritual aspect.

As there are many ways that stress affects your health and brings you out of harmony, it's important to work at releasing the stress from your life. I know it's not easy if you have a full and active life, juggling work, parenting and other responsibilities. However, a whole industry has grown up nowadays around the controlling and managing of stress, so there are lots of therapies and remedies available. There are also many things we can do for ourselves to alleviate this anxiety. Here are several key 'starters' for relieving stress:

✧ Develop a positive mindset.

✧ Feed yourself and exercise your body well.

✧ When stress overcomes you, take time to breathe deeply and slowly.

✧ Get in touch with nature.

✧ Work on gratitude.

We are given so much encouragement in the twenty-first century to be on the go 24/7 and to accumulate material wealth and possessions. For some people, this may be exactly what they need to do, but for each of us it will be different. We need to examine what makes us feel 'rich' and 'blessed' in our lives, both in material possessions and in the many other enjoyments life has to offer.

Healing stress

Here's a short exercise from stress therapist Annie Lawler, which she finds extremely effective with her clients. Everyone has time to do this exercise. It can be done when you wake up in the morning, before you go to bed at night, sitting on a bus or train (but not in the car!), while taking a walk or when taking it easy.

Exercise to release stress

✧ Make a list of all the things that are good in your life at the moment. Spend ten minutes or so studying it and focusing on all these good things. Perhaps it's relationships (friends, family, partners, etc.); maybe it's your work, a talent you may have, your home, a new car or some other good fortune. At times it may be difficult to remember what is good, but even then, if you think about the basics such as whether you have access to running water, regular food and secure shelter, these are more than many have and are certainly good things. You may also want to be grateful for things like your health, your appearance, your education or your freedom of speech and travel. Mother nature also gives us a lot to be grateful for – although we often forget to notice. Think of the trees and things that spring from the earth – the colour, the scents, the materials with which we can build shelters and make clothes, the healing qualities of herbs and plants, the foods and so on. The more you think about it, the more the list may grow.

✧ Some days you may choose to add to the list or simply to sit and look at it. If you're somewhere outdoors, you may just want to run through the list in your mind. But whatever you choose to focus on, make sure you concentrate on the positives. Notice what happens around you and how you feel when you practise this simple exercise daily.

✧ Until the next time, be positive and take care of yourself.

Thank you, Annie

SUPPRESSED EMOTIONS

*Blocked emotions hold negative and dense energies
locked inside, which although hidden will prevent a
full and constant spiritual and soul connection.*

Apart from stress, the other major danger with emotions is suppression. Suppressing your emotions, not giving voice to how you feel, can be incredibly harmful on a day-to-day basis. It's a potential time bomb that can explode into illness at any time. If, like the child, you speak out when you feel upset then you can let go your negative emotions before they harm you. Of course, throwing toys out of prams and stamping your feet will only get a negative response from those around you, but a gentle and firm expression of your feelings is greatly beneficial and far better than the British stiff upper lip approach.

You may keep quiet to save the feelings of others, to avoid confrontation, to keep the peace, to avoid embarrassment. Or maybe you find it difficult to express what you feel. However, it truly is the best policy to 'let it out' rather than 'keep it in'. How can people react, work or live with you if they do not know what you feel and how you are reacting to their actions, words and attitudes?

Do you express your feelings in the following circumstances:

✧ When you feel marginalised and ignored?

✧ When you feel left out by friends or work colleagues?

✧ When you are criticised, in your perception, unjustly?

✧ When you have been treated unfairly?

✧ When your actions have been misunderstood?

✧ When someone tries to bulldoze your ideas and plans?

✧ When your partner selects their TV choices rather than yours once too often?

✧ When your ideas are blocked?

✧ When your heart is broken by grief at the loss of a dear one?

✧ When you are rejected in love?

✧ When you are rejected at work and someone else gets the promotion?

If you don't speak out in circumstances like these, then you need to focus both on releasing old emotions that are left over from past experiences and on expressing your current feelings. I will shortly lead you through a way of releasing the old baggage you carry, because it will be keeping you out of balance and will seriously affect your overall holistic harmony.

EMOTIONS AFFECT YOUR THOUGHTS AND ATTITUDES

Mr Mental often takes a bashing from Mr Emotional and the two can work together to create disharmony and distress for the mind. For example, between them they create agoraphobia – the fear of going out and about; and claustrophobia – the fear of being in confined places. In fact they can create insecurity on many levels, inspiring fearful thoughts about your financial security, whether your partner will leave you, whether you will fail at your job or be made redundant, and a myriad others. Your fears and anxieties and other negative emotions can also create attitudes that affect your character and personality, so that you may become irritable, angry and short-tempered with those around you. This in turn will affect the way they treat you. So we have another cause of disharmony between your component parts: your emotions making waves for your personality.

EMOTIONS CAN SERIOUSLY AFFECT YOUR HEALTH – WATCH OUT, MR PHYSICAL!

There is more than one way in which the physical body can become the victim of an emotional body that is out of control. We have seen how stress can affect your physical body. In addition, the energy of your thoughts affects the life force energy that flows through your physical body. A stream of negative thoughts about a particular worry will condense as an energy block – we call that a negative thought form. Thought forms block the natural flow of energy through your body and a lack of energy in any organ can cause illness and disease. Remember, your body gets a fair amount of abuse from the rest of the pack, especially from Mr Emotional. A good reason then to focus on healing this unseen but deeply felt aspect of who you are.

Before we look at some more of the negative aspects of our emotions and how to heal and manage them, let's consider the positive aspects and cheer ourselves up a little. Let's see what our goal should be – to create and bring ourselves to the point where we live with positive and uplifting emotions.

POSITIVE EMOTIONAL CONDITIONS

These are the feelings that you want to encourage. Focus on what brings up these feelings for you and get more of them!

✧ **Joy**. Feelings of joy will uplift your spirits, energise your body and send your mind off into the realm of positive, hopeful, inspirational thoughts.

✧ **Peace** in your emotions will make you feel contented and calm your mind, stopping it constantly whizzing around, looking for things to worry about.

✧ **Gratitude**. Feelings of gratitude will expand you spiritually and open the door to abundance. Being thankful comes from an inner acceptance without criticism of what you have. This combination of senses and thoughts is a powerful force to bring contentment.

✧ **Ecstasy** is a high vibration emotion that comes from time to time when you feel the full force of spiritual and divine presence. I have experienced this on many occasions; it is an indescribable and wonderful feeling that brings a profound belief that you are connected to something quite amazing.

✧ **Love** is the emotion that will make the greatest changes in your life. Without love you will not be able to heal the wounds of the past or open to the wonders of spirit.

Now let's remind ourselves of the way in which negative emotions can affect us, whether current or suppressed from the past, and why we need to heal them in order to harmonise our whole self:

✧ Negative feelings trigger negative thoughts that create energy blocks, affecting the flow of energising life force to all the organs and all aspects of the physical body.

✧ Fears and anxieties send negative charges that weaken the immune system, deplete your energy and affect your spirits, causing depression and creating illnesses and ailments for the physical body.

✧ Anger can eat away and disturb your equilibrium, break up relationships and aggravate everyone around you.

✧ Holding on to the past can make you bitter, eating away at you mentally and physically and upsetting your inter-personal relationships. It can trap you in the past where pain revisits you.

✧ Pessimism affects you mentally and drags you down.

✧ Lack of self-love can trigger thoughts of self-hatred, fuelling the spiral of low self-esteem and self-confidence that can seriously block and slow down your journey.

Sometimes it's difficult to see whether it's your thoughts or your emotions that are the main culprit for the disturbance of your inner peace and the creation of stressful feelings. But if you work on healing and harmonising both your mind and your emotions, you will bring the sense of peace and calm you need to clear the way to your connection with your Higher Self and the more permanent state of peace that this will bring.

Harmony and inner peace are a platform for your connection.

HEALING YOUR EMOTIONS AND ENCOURAGING THEM TO BE POSITIVE

It's important for your intention of bringing yourself into harmony to release, manage and control your stress, anxiety, anger, bitterness and other negative emotions. Even if you don't identify that you are actually suffering from any of these, you may have suppressed feelings that are affecting you at a deep level. So I suggest you use this exercise to give yourself an emotional spring clean!

Releasing old suppressed emotions

This is an exercise that I have shared with my readers previously and used many times in workshops and healing intensives, so you may already have gone through this process. But you hold so much captive in your cellular memory and deep within that it is something you can do time and time and again, letting go layer upon layer of the past – like an onion – that holds levels of old pain. The other great reason for including it is that IT WORKS! This simple process will go a long way to help you to heal anger and bitterness, the guilt and self-doubt caused by past actions.

✧ Find a quiet place, take a pad of writing paper and have plenty of tissues to hand.

✧ Allow yourself a trip into your past. Focus on the painful experiences you find there and the people who have hurt you. Think of each person individually.

✧ Write a final letter to each person, telling them about the pain and suffering they caused you. Share your feelings and don't hold anything back – they will never read this but it will be most cathartic for you to write it all down.

✧ If you failed to share your love with someone who has passed on, then write a love letter to them – let it go now. If they are in spirit, they will sense your love and receive it.

✧ Hold the intention that this is the final time you are going to relive these hurtful feelings.

✧ Tear the letters up and burn them. Watch the flames turn the negative feelings into light, transforming the energy and releasing your old feelings.

✧ Now send thoughts of forgiveness to all those that have harmed you. This will counteract the bitterness you feel.

As well as carrying out this exercise, there are various ways in which you can help bring your emotional body into balance. By managing your time – giving yourself more time – you will be able to diminish pressure and stress. By prioritising your goals and workload you can take the stress out by enabling yourself to focus on one thing at a time. In addition you might like to take up some powerful, relaxing pastimes. These include:

✧ **Yoga** – a time-honoured exercise for mind, body and spirit
✧ **Pilates** – a gentle and powerful way to release tension and emotional charge
✧ **Tai chi** – controlled physical exercise that creates focus and releases tension

✧ **Meditation** – creating time for stillness and introspection will calm your emotions and body
✧ **Deep breathing** – calms anxieties and lowers the heartbeat enforcing a state of peace
✧ **Reiki** – hands-on energy healing, extremely beneficial for achieving calm and relaxation
✧ **Chiro Kinetic Therapy (CKT)** – identifies the source of emotional disturbance
✧ **Massage** – a good massage will take away tension, especially if you use essential oils

As we go through this book I will be taking you deeper into the healing process and we will look for the root cause of your emotional problems, finding what is behind the symptoms. Often it's not your choice to feel angry, to hold on to the past, to be affected by fears and anxieties. These emotions can be caused by the wounds and imprints of past experiences. We will address these in order to ensure that the root as well as the visible aspect of your problems is cleared. In the meantime, daily work on positive attitudes, gratitude, sharing your thoughts and feelings and caring about yourself will take you a long way towards your goal of connection with your Higher Self.

SPIRITUAL BODY – YOUR SOUL AND SPIRIT

Your spiritual body is made up of the aspects of spirit that are unique to you – your soul, your monad and your spirit. Your spirit is the stream of divine energy that flows from Divine Source through your monad. It is the energy of love that revitalises and uplifts you. When you are not fully connected, this can be sporadic and come and go in its intensity. It can be a stream of pure love or can be affected by the vibration of your own energy.

If you're full of anger, or lacking love either for yourself or others, if you're holding guilt or are shut down to the concept that you have a spiritual aspect and to God, then the flow of your spirit can be reduced, or may be contaminated by the negativity you hold. This negativity will take your spirit from pure love and high vibration energy down to a lower, more negative, heavier vibration. It's the difference between a person who is energised and vibrant, who radiates love, life, light and optimism, and someone who is tired, downbeat, depressive, despondent and downcast, and who drains the energies of those around them. Once you are fully connected your spirit will be strong and definable and will be the source of the joyous feelings and bliss that are your goal.

Just for the record, the Bible says that God made man in his own image (not a expression we feminists feel too happy about!). I believe that statement refers to the fact that your soul and monad – your Higher Self – is made of the same essence as God and the spirit that flows through you and from you is the equivalent of the Holy Spirit. Of course, the Holy Spirit is totally pure; it is pure love and hence is the most beautiful and uplifting energy stream in the universe. If you have ever felt it you will know of its healing power and the ecstasy that it brings.

As your spirit sits within you it takes on the form of your physical body and creates what we call the etheric body, reflecting all the other bodies, emotional, mental and physical. When you die your etheric body should go with your soul back through your silver cord to the higher planes of heaven. As I explained in Chapter 1, your soul is the unique spiritual energy form that travels to earth and joins your body for its earthly journey of experience. It holds imprints of good and bad experiences from the past. It was created from love and its wish and desire is to return to that state.

Your soul is desperate to be healed and become whole again. When you suffer great pain – either emotional or mental pain or a combination of mental, emotional and physical pain – your soul can be wounded. For example, if you are stabbed to death by someone you trust, you will feel not only the physical pain but also the emotional pain of betrayal. If you commit suicide and your soul realises that you have caused huge grief and despair to your loved ones, you will feel immense guilt. If you have been abused by a parent or close relative, you will feel mental and emotional pain and lose trust. These situations can wound your soul.

In Chapter 7 I shall be expanding on the role of the soul: how it is damaged by earthly experiences, how it heals itself and how it can be healed. But I would just mention here that it uses the physical body to take on its pain and hurt. Some ailments and illnesses are caused by the overflow of the pain of the soul as it tries to release the negative energies that it holds; these are often skin complaints like eczema and sclerosis. In my healing I always focus on the soul, for as the soul heals so all the other bodies release their negativity and heal. As long as the illness has not been too degenerative, this includes the physical body.

A spiritual body that is evolved and free from pain:

✧ Exudes joy, radiating light and love.

✧ Is free and unfettered.

✧ Is light and uplifting for those around.

✧ Heals through the pure energy that it channels and radiates.

✧ Can be seen through the eyes, which will sparkle and shine.

✧ Helps and assists the physical body rather than burdens it.

✧ Passes wisdom to the mental body and inspires it.

A spiritual body that holds wounds and pain:

✧ Will affect the mental body, causing depression, mental illness, negative thoughts.

✧ Will affect the emotional body, becoming the unknown cause of anxiety and fear.

✧ Will affect the physical body, causing unexplained tiredness, ailments and diseases that cannot be cured with traditional medicine.

✧ Can cause mood swings that affect your character and your attitudes to others.

✧ Will push you to find a way to heal it, inspiring you to find alternative therapies or holistic healing, drawing you to a spiritual healer, taking you into situations that give you the opportunity to grow and heal (these will seem like bad luck, negative circumstances and accidents but will all be driven from your soul's determination to heal).

✧ Will crave love, both from your world and from the divine, driving your desire to follow a spiritual path or bringing you close to nature in an attempt to get you to open your heart.

By looking at the spiritual body we are going down a layer to the deeper causes of your problems. You can see that some of your confusion, pain and disharmony have underlying spiritual causes. If your soul holds wounds and imprints from past experiences, from this lifetime or others, then all other aspects of yourself may be affected. That is why we will be working on these deep, core problems throughout the book.

EGO – YOUR SENSE OF SELF

Your ego is your sense of self and your value of self – in other words, if you think you are worthy or not. If you have a positive and balanced ego, you have a healthy acceptance of what you are, what you can achieve and your value to yourself and society. You will be easy to live with and unlikely to upset other aspects of self.

A negative ego can swing two ways. If you have an inflated ego you may tend to think you are better than you are, you may be inclined to boastfulness and arrogance. In common use this is the ego that we often refer to when we say someone is egotistical; we say they have a large ego or an inflated ego. However, I have found there are many more people with underdeveloped egos, who do not value them-selves enough and who suffer from low self-esteem as a result.

In your quest to know yourself it would be very useful if you could look at your ego and search for the reasons that it may be out of balance. The way your parents and teachers responded to you is often the cause, but you may have a very self-critical nature and you may also have been told to be humble – which is not necessarily a good thing. Excessive humility can cause you to develop a negative ego where you say all the time 'I can't' or 'I'm not good enough'. It may also drive you to try to prove yourself. This can be a problem too, if your drive and determination to prove yourself is paranoid or excessive and if you are never satisfied with what you achieve. Your ego is the way you see yourself and its positive or negative status can affect your entire life!

The following simple exercise will help bring your ego into balance:

Exercise to bring the ego into balance

✧ Sit down in a quiet spot.

✧ Say to yourself gently but firmly: *'I am perfectly fine exactly as I am – I accept and approve of myself. I am what I need to be at this precise moment in time. All changes and healing are for my greatest good and they will come at the perfect time.'*

This will help you to stop the constant barrage of self-criticism and will leave you open to healing all other aspects of yourself, which in itself will bring you towards contentment with yourself.

One of the impacts of an inflated ego is that you are in danger of working without spirit, without God, without recognising your spiritual self. Hence the expression Edging God Out. To help bring your ego into balance, make a point to ask Source, the Universe, God or the Angels – or any spiritual being that you have an affinity with – to assist you in all you do. See your work, whatever it is, as a joint venture with Spirit.

PHYSICAL BODY: THE VEHICLE FOR YOUR HOLISTIC SELF

You will have seen that your physical body is the part of you that gets the most damage from the rest of the gang! The body is the last component to show the discord, and, in some cases, the most seriously affected. Often we do not respond to our own needs – allow ourselves to relax and unwind; give up a job that doesn't suit us; walk away from an abusive relationship; speak up about unfair treatment; stop pushing ourselves; give ourselves a good diet and sleep – until we have a physical symptom that we can no longer ignore. You may already have experienced early warning signs that all is not well. But very likely you have ignored them – most of us do! Don't wait until the indigestion becomes an ulcer, the high blood pressure becomes a heart attack or the tension and pressure causes one of your organs to fail.

What can you do about this? Well, as you heal, the different aspects of your body will be less and less likely to feel the discomfort and pain caused by mental and emotional disharmony and discord. As you combat and manage your negativity, anger and bitterness and calm your mind, so your body will not need to announce the imbalance to you through illness. As you become more and more in touch with your Higher Self and your spiritual essence, the need for disease will disappear.

RESPECT YOUR BODY

Your body has a spirit of its own. An extremely valuable practice is to speak to your body's spirit and show it respect. Say to your body 'I am sorry for the pressure I have put you under.' Tell it that you love it and respect it. Thank it for holding the negative energies created by other aspects of your being. Then put those good intentions of respecting and loving your body into action:

✧ Eat a nourishing and healthy diet, avoiding processed foods, fat and sugar.

✧ Get plenty of fresh air and exercise – choose something to do that you enjoy.

✧ Drink plenty of clean water – eight glasses a day would be a good goal.

✧ Take rest – take holidays, take time out each day just to be calm and relax. This is important for all aspects of you, but your body will particularly appreciate it.

✧ Listen to the signs – your body will tell you when it's flagging, when the mind has given it too many tasks to achieve.

✧ Don't let the ego make you say yes to everything and everyone. Learn to say no.

✧ When your emotions are on overload, take time to let them out – let them be expressed – before they turn inwards and start to act as poison to your body.

SOUL AND GENES MEET

Now let's look for a moment at the connection between our soul and our physical body. This will complete the picture of who you are – the combination of spiritual history and genetic history. As I mentioned earlier, your soul joins your physical form at the time of your birth. It may even visit a few times while you are in your mother's womb. I have seen a spirit fluttering around a room when healing a pregnant woman, and both she and I had the sense that it was her baby's soul coming to see what was going on! From the moment our soul unites with our body each of us becomes a fully fledged person. We operate in all senses and have spiritual awareness. Through our highest spiritual aspect, we hold in our cellular memory – the memory held in the cells of our body and which comes with us when we are born – everything that our own soul has experienced and learnt and everything our clan, family, tribe and race has experienced. This includes the attitudes, tendencies and characteristics that pass from generation to generation.

In this life, from the day we are born we are affected by the past experiences of our soul and of our ancestors.

Every illness and life-challenging deprivation will be in our genes. Every strength gained through overcoming these physical challenges will also be in our genes. The food our ancestors ate will affect our genes; so will the air that they breathed, the way that they farmed, their proximity to mountains or the sea, their social and communal activities. Even their beliefs and emotional traits will come through into our genes. Let's look at the different ways in which the experiences of those long-ago predecessors in our family tree can affect us, and then at what we can do about it. Many of the things that you experience are inherited – here are a few of them.

GENETICALLY AFFECTED DISABILITIES

Many of the illnesses, disorders and disabilities that you may be born with have a direct genetic cause. There are 7,000 recorded genetic diseases, some of which are more common than others. The most common disorder is coeliac disease or intolerance to gluten, which affects the digestive system. I am sure you know at least one person with this, or with its milder form, wheat intolerance.

First let's focus on the disabilities that are caused by damage to the mother's egg. A woman's eggs are resident in her body and fully formed for years and are therefore vulnerable to damage. If a woman is affected by any form of radiation, by chemicals or other toxic substances, even by viruses, then her eggs can be affected too. Sometimes this manifests in a baby born with severe genetic disorder. Serious disorders of this kind include Thalidomide impairment, Down's syndrome and cystic fibrosis – life-debilitating conditions which bring huge challenges for those that suffer from them and their families.

I give healing to adults and children with these problems, but I focus on the emotional fallout experienced by close family members. Currently I have no effective tools for healing the disorders themselves, although as I step through my limitations I hope that if it becomes appropriate, more extensive healing will take place. In the meantime I offer love and acceptance, which can be healing as balm to the heart and soul – especially for children who have abnormalities that make them different from other children. In some communities their differences are the cause of shame and may be such a taboo that these children are shut away. In such circumstances I hope that through my unconditional love for the children, I can help their parents overcome the cultural barriers, enabling them to be proud of their children and love them too. I also focus on healing the stress that parents experience in supporting their disabled or chronically ill children.

From your perspective, with your intention of reaching your spiritual goal, these illnesses will not be barriers. The way you cope with them, for yourself and for those around you, can in fact give you inner strength and accelerate your spiritual evolution. They will in all circumstances be part of your divine plan, although that might not be a helpful thing to point out to someone who is suffering. I would like to say here that the idea that such an illness is a punishment for a wrong action in a previous life is incorrect. Karma can however lead you to take on the burden of an illness in order to understand it better, to gain empathy for those who are physically disabled or to show courage in adversity. This is not a punishment from God.

A close and dear friend of mine has a daughter with cerebral palsy. She is an absolute sweetheart and she lifts the spirits of everyone who meets her with her sunny disposition, her determination to be as independent as possible and her inner strength. With her strong spirit she has overcome the challenges of her illness, which has left her unable to walk, talk coherently or support herself. You probably know a similar role model in your family or community, someone who is struggling with a major disadvantage but shows strength of character, determination and the ability to smile and enjoy life.

TENDENCIES TOWARDS CERTAIN ILLNESSES

Other diseases are not themselves genetic in origin but may be prevalent in your family and ancestral history. There are a number of illnesses that run in families, for example cancer, heart disease, arthritis, asthma and diabetes. You can hold a susceptibility to these illnesses and diseases in your genes – even baldness can come in this group! When you take out health insurance you will be asked about the existence of such illnesses in your family history, for according to the statistics there is a risk that you will follow the family trend.

However, although you may have a natural inclination towards one of these physical weaknesses it doesn't mean that you have to follow in your family's footsteps. On my mother's side there is a predisposition to arthritis. My grandfather was chair-bound with it, my uncle had a hip replacement and my mother has had both hips replaced. Twenty years ago I also had the beginnings of arthritis in my hips and found walking on uneven ground very painful. I decided not to follow the family. Having researched the physical and spiritual causes of arthritis, I subsequently avoided the foods that can aggravate the illness; I gave up red meat – in fact for the last twelve years I have been a vegetarian – and I have made regular exercise a feature of my life. I discovered the link between mental and emotional attitudes and thought forms and disease. A self-critical mindset can encourage arthritis, so I focused on healing this with self-acceptance and tolerance. Thank goodness, I now have no signs of the illness whatsoever.

FAMILY TRAITS

Remember that you chose which race, which country and which family would suit your particular aims for your current lifetime. Although you may feel you have weaknesses that are inherited – you may even feel the victim of these at times – there will be a reason why you chose them. You may be looking for a challenge, for if you overcome these weaknesses then you will grow.

You may be able to use the gifts that you have inherited from your parents to help you with your own mission. For example, if you come from a family of orators you may inherit their ability to speak up. If you are to help bring changes to the world and teach new ways, this will be a great gift for you. You may pick up these skills and gifts from your parents or from your grandparents, as they often skip a generation. Of course, some of your gifts and strengths come from your own personal soul/spirit and have nothing to do with your genes. You will know – so let's look at some of the positive and negative attributes you may inherit:

✧ Being a worrier – I'm often informed with a grimace, 'Unfortunately, I get that from my mum'.

✧ Introvert or extravert. If your parents are shy and retiring it will affect you in two ways – either you will inherit that trait or you will go the opposite way and become bold and outgoing.

✧ Packing a temper. Another expression I hear often is 'I've got my father's temper'.

✧ Artistic, acting and musical abilities.

✧ Physical strengths and skills.

Exercise

This exercise will help you focus on the aspects that you have inherited from your parents and to see how they have helped you in your life's journey, either as challenges (giving you an opportunity to grow) or as skills and attributes to enable you to meet your life's purpose.

✧ Write down all the gifts and strengths that you feel you have inherited from your family.

✧ See how these have helped you in your life's work. Have you considered the weaknesses a hindrance? Could you heal any of them? Is there any way you could maximise the strengths and gifts to further your own work or enhance your life?

HEALING YOUR GENETIC STREAM

I will now share with you the way that I heal any negative charge that has been passed down through the generations and is affecting you adversely in the present. Any such imprint will have affected the cells of your body and will hold the memory of the past. So how can we heal someone who is no longer here? Isn't this healing the past? Yes, it is.

To understand how this works I must tell you a little about time. In the world of spirit – in the higher dimensions of life, the astral planes and the higher realms – time runs in cycles, not in a straight line as it does on the denser planes of Earth. You may find this hard to digest, but suffice to say that time outside this earthly experience does not consist of one situation followed by another in the sequential way we see it here. This means that we can focus on a situation – such as the wounding of a soul or group of souls – and heal it as though it is going on in front of us. It is in this way that I heal the past. I focus on the situation, the problem of the past, and see it as though it is happening now. So the souls of those already dead can be healed, as can situations that have happened in this and previous lifetimes. The healing releases the negative energy, loves and uplifts the spirit and calms the emotions.

Exercise to heal the genetic stream

You can follow this process for yourself or for a friend. You will notice that you will be asking permission from the souls involved before you go ahead. You will be giving the option for the healing to be ignored or for the love to be used in whichever way the soul chooses. This prevents you from over-riding the soul's free will.

✧ Find a quiet place – you do not want to be disturbed while you do this.

✧ If you are performing the process for yourself, sit in front of a mirror. You will then be using your reflection as the focus of your healing. If you are doing it for a friend, have them sit facing you.

✧ Focus on the problem that you feel has an inherited source.

✧ Say *'I ask permission to heal and release the karma of all my ancestors, back to the source of my problem. If you decline, please use the love in whichever way you choose. Please take this love and healing and use it for the highest good of all.'*

✧ Now say *'It is my intention to release all blocks, karma, imprints and wounds that have been passed to me in my DNA.'* Ask for help from your angels, spirit guides or any spiritual or religious figure that you respect and wish to include.

✧ Protect your energy field by seeing yourself surrounded by a violet flame, gold light or any other protection you wish.

✧ Focus on the left hand side of the figure opposite you (that will be your reflection in the mirror or your friend), looking to the right. This represents the mother. Say '*Accept this love for your healing and release your karma, now.*'

✧ Then focus on the right hand side, looking to the left. This represents the father. Say '*Accept this love for your healing and release your karma, now.*'

✧ Now draw the genetic healing symbol in front of you, imagining you are facing the entire family tree. Draw it three times upwards with two hands. As you draw the symbol, say '*I release and dissolve all blocks, imprints and karma through the generations back to source.*'

Genetic healing symbol

✧ Then sweep your hands down through the family tree, saying *'I send love and healing through each generation, through me and my children and my children's children.'* Do this three times.

As doctors and scientists work on eliminating the more disastrous effects of some genetic conditions, we can continue to use healing to alleviate the effects on us emotionally and utilise our strengths to their maximum effect.

As your body becomes free of the impact of your other aspects, harmony returns - when harmony is restored you come closer to your goal of connection.

Meditation to bring yourself into balance and harmony

Here is an exercise you can do to encourage the harmony of all your different facets. This exercise uses the power of your will and intention to make changes. Through visualisation and intention to change, you are sending messages to all aspects of yourself to be aware of each other and to act in a way that is supportive rather than harmful, for example to ask the mind to stop going back to past painful experiences which set the emotions off on a replay.

✧ In a quiet place, sit comfortably, drop your shoulders and relax your body.

✧ See yourself as a huge tree. See your roots growing deep into the ground, stabilising, strengthening and grounding.

✦ Now visualise the various parts that make up the total you – see them as miniatures of you if you wish, or look at the illustration of our holistic bodies at the beginning of this chapter. If you can't visualise, know that you are focusing on:

✦ your mental body
✦ your emotional body
✦ your spiritual body
✦ your character and ego
✦ your physical body

✦ Out loud ask your mental body, emotional body, spiritual body, physical body, character and ego to be aware of each other, to show respect and love to each other, to work in harmony together for your greater good. Thank them for all the love they hold and the energy they have given you, and for the support that they show already.

✦ See these beautiful beings linking and creating a ring of love and friendship. See a beautiful spiral of light linking and joining all the aspects that make you who you are. See the light getting brighter and brighter as they link together and your life force energy flows stronger and stronger.

✦ Know that you are in balance and in harmony.

Bless you.

So now I hope you can see some of the impact of the various components and aspects of yourself upon one another and how they interconnect for good and bad. I suggest you continue to work on all aspects of yourself, practise the exercises, keep yourself as relaxed as you can. Keep the intention to be aware of how the various parts of you act as a group venture, working together for the good of the whole and travelling in unison. As every aspect of you becomes positive and vibrant, so you as a whole are in a state to co-join again with your higher vibration – your Higher Self. Once you are connected to this aspect of you, pure, unconditional love can become part of you every minute of every day and you will feel great all the time!

Having seen how the internal and personal aspects of you can be brought into a calm and peaceful state, let's now look at how the influences of those around us can take us off course.

Remember who you are - a creator, created from the greatest creator.

FIVE

Releasing Negativity

All energies, thoughts and feelings that are not of love will take you further and further from your goal of being fully connected to your Higher Self.

I will now start to take you through the healing of the blocks and limitations that prevent you from feeling your divinity and allowing the energy of your Higher Self to flow through you and your life. In the last chapter we looked at the mind and how negative thoughts can affect our total harmony. In this chapter I would like to go further into the effects that negative energies can have on you. I will address how negative energies create blocks around us – energies created by our thoughts, belief systems, fears, responsibilities, other people's expectations, demands and dependency. The outer layer of negative energies that come from thoughts and attitudes, moods and emotions are a little like a coat that we can shed.

NEGATIVE ENERGY

In the truest sense of the word there is no negative energy, but there is energy that is heavy, unlike the light and vibrant energy of love. We could call it loveless energy. However, to keep things simple and straightforward I shall use the term 'negative energy' to describe any atmosphere or energy that you create or attract that pulls you down and keeps you away from your Higher Self. Each day we pick up energies and attachments and create blocks and heaviness in our energy field. There are a number of sources of negativity and I will address those that most commonly affect us.

YOUR OWN FEARS, ANXIETIES AND WORRIES

First, I should point out that you are a moving mass of tiny specks of energy. Although you feel dense (not in your mind of course!) and solid, you are in fact far from it. Compared to the invisible energies around you, you are more solid and hold a visible form, but you are made up of energy. Because of this you are susceptible to the changing vibrations of the energies around you.

You are also affected by your own thoughts and feelings. Positive thoughts make your overall energy lighter and raise its frequency, while negative thoughts hold a heavier and denser vibration. Therefore the more upbeat and positive you feel, the lighter becomes your energy; the more despondent and unhappy you are, the heaver and darker your overall energy becomes.

Apart from this overall effect, negative thoughts like anger, resentment, self-dislike, pessimism and anxiety will create actual blocks in your energy field. When you have the same negative thought about yourself or your life over and over again, the energies of these thoughts bind together and create a mass that obstructs the flow of energy through your system. Thoughts like:

'I hate my body'
'I don't know where the rent money is coming from'
'I don't have enough clients – I fear my business will fail'
'I wonder if this lump is cancer'
'I am so scared of dying'
'I am useless – my mother was right'

All these will stay with you and bring you down, spiritually, emotionally and physically.

Thought forms created from anxious and negative thoughts

Keep your thoughts positive and your energy levels will rise and you will uplift your spirits. Avoid creating negative thought forms.

THE EFFECTS OF NEGATIVE BLOCKS

As your life force energy struggles to flow through and around these blocks it becomes sluggish. This in itself affects how you feel: you will become tired easily and find yourself collapsing exhausted on the sofa at the end of the day – that's even if you make it to the evening! This is an area of your wellbeing that you can control by ensuring that you keep your thoughts positive.

I believe that this is a matter of programming and habit. Every time you catch yourself making a negative comment about yourself or saying something pessimistic about your future, stop yourself and say something positive and uplifting to clear it. Eventually you will train yourself to look on the upside of everything that happens to you. Remember that your journey is one of learning and growing, so even the bad experiences give you a lesson to learn.

THE LAW OF ATTRACTION

Another reason for avoiding negative thoughts is that you attract to you what you visualise. As you send out a picture, an energy form of what you fear, so you create a magnet that draws towards you the very thing that is making you anxious. This is the spiritual law of attraction in action. You get what you ask for, you create with your thoughts – taking thought to matter, you draw to you what you desire. This law can work for your benefit – we will look at the positive working of the power of manifesting and creating at the end of this book – but just now be sure that you are not drawing towards you the very thing you fear.

It's absolutely essential that you keep your thoughts as positive as you possibly can. If they start to run away with you, write down your positive intentions or draw yourself smiling (stick men drawings will do just fine). Find a photo of yourself when you were carefree and happy and stick it on your fridge to remind you of how it felt. Focus on smiling. When your friends ring, tell them honestly how you feel but don't keep repeating the bad news – say what is going on for you then move on to something more uplifting. Otherwise you are in danger of reinforcing the negative charge around you.

Clearing and releasing negative thought forms

Here is a process that works very well to clear and lighten your energy field. The principle we are using here is that you are dispersing the balls of negative energy that cling to each other like a magnet. These are your negative thoughts, which are drawn like to like to create blocks. Negativity from other people will be attracted in the same way. Once you release your negativity you will find you are not a magnet for outside negativity either.

✧ Find a quiet place and shut the door – even if this is the loo at work. You don't want people thinking you have lost the plot!

✧ Use your hands as combs. Sweep and comb through your energy field and flick away the energies – this will disperse them.

✧ Hold the intention of lightening your energy field and clearing all that is not supporting and lifting you. If you are completely alone, say '*I release all negativity that is in and attached to my aura.*'

✧ If you are in your own home it's useful to flick the unwanted energies into a bowl of water and sea salt, for salt attracts and holds negativity and it will help to keep your room clear.

Exercise to release fears

If you have a persistent fear that troubles you constantly, you may find this exercise useful. Remember that these negative thoughts are dragging you away from your goal. The more work you do to release them, the faster you will reconnect and hold the connection.

✧ First identify the fear. Write it down. Do you remember when you started to be aware of it and what caused it? Are there any particular situations or people that trigger the fear? Understanding the cause and what it is can be the beginning of taking your power back over it. Currently it's dominating your life and your goal is to be the master of it.

✧ You may also be attached to your fear through the habit that it has formed in you – in other words, thinking of it constantly links you to it through the energy stream of your thoughts. It was created in the past and needs to be left there, so the next step is to go through the letting-go exercise I gave you in Chapter 4.

✧ You now need to reprogramme your mind to think positively and to release its tendency to brood and keep creating
more negative thoughts to fuel it. Write a mantra – a positive affirmation that contradicts the fear that you have. For
example, if you are fearful of leaving the house, say '*I am
free to go where I choose – this is my right and my free will.*'

Next we will look at the way other people's negativity can
affect you, and how to avoid being pulled down by it.

OTHER PEOPLE'S NEGATIVE THOUGHTS

In my book *Healing Negative Energies* I deal in depth with
how other people's energies affect us and how you can protect
yourself from them. But I will cover the basic points about
this again here, as it's most important that you keep yourself
strong against the downbeat thoughts and attitudes of others.
In some instances people may make deliberate efforts to
'bring you down' because of rivalry or jealousy. As we know,
thoughts are streams of energy. If the emotion that connects
to a thought is negative, then the person who is the focus
of that thought will feel the effect. This can bring a person
down emotionally, energetically and ultimately physically. This
sort of negativity can be created by a range of thoughts, from
office gossip through to intentional curses and the use of
black magic. Just spending time in a crowded place like a
railway station, airport or busy shopping mall may affect how
you feel, especially if you are sensitive to these energies.

AVOIDING OTHERS' NEGATIVE THOUGHTS

Clearing and healing old wounds and the heavy, sticky energy you generate from your own fears and guilt will prevent you from being a magnet for other people's negativity. We will be looking at these deeper wounds soon and how you can heal them. This will take time and work, so in the meantime, as you clear yourself, you may find it helpful to protect yourself against outside energies. There are a number of techniques – here are just a few:

✧ Visualise yourself surrounded by a violet flame of protective energy. This also clears both other people's thought forms and your own.

✧ Use the protection symbol overleaf, which was given to me by my spirit guide. Simply draw it in front of you three times. You can also wear it as a talisman in the form of a piece of jewellery (my company Ripple makes pendants and earrings and also an essential oil blend for protection – see the back of the book for details).

✧ See yourself in a bubble of light that has thick walls which nothing but love can enter – all the emotional shafts that come to you bounce off the walls.

✧ Surround your home, workstation, car, group of friends on a night out or just yourself with a blue ring of light.

✧ If you are under a really nasty attack, call in Archangel Michael, an amazing spiritual being whose intention is to protect us mere mortals. Just ask him to protect you and he will be with you.

✧ Certain crystals hold the energy vibrations that will create a shield around you. Obsidian and tourmaline are just two that have this effect.

✧ Ask God, the angels or any spiritual guide or master that you believe in to help you.

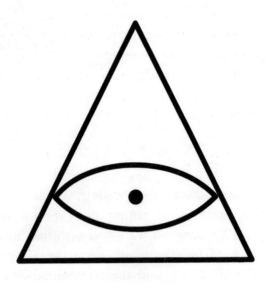

Protection symbol

It's also important to hold yourself in strength and believe you will be unaffected by others. Spiritual strength comes as you clear the imprints and negative effects of your past. I find it much easier to stay strong since I have worked on releasing my anxieties, and I have seen many of my clients become spiritually much stronger and less fearful as they heal and make their connections stronger.

CURSES AND BLACK MAGIC

There are situations where people deliberately use negative energies to cause harm and disruption. Since I started healing twelve years ago I have specialised in helping people who suffer from black magic, curses, possession and psychic attack. In Asia and Africa it is not unusual to have clients who believe they are the victims of black magic or that they have been cursed. In a way this is understandable, as there are sangomas and witchdoctors working very actively to use the dark forces and demons against people. They make a living casting spells and curses for money.

In the West we don't really expect to be cursed by a business rival or a jealous sibling. However, curses can be passed down through families and carried from one life to the next. I have a client who booked for a healing session over the phone. Even before she came I had a sense that she had been through a lot. When she spoke on the phone I thought I had made a mistake – this upbeat, positive, strong voice could surely not belong to a woman who had gone through such a difficult life. But it was her. I warmed to her instantly and as we talked I felt a creepy energy moving along my back. I asked her if she had ever considered that she might be cursed. At this she broke down – with relief. She was so happy that I had confirmed her own idea that this was the case.

Once we both acknowledged that she was being affected by outside forces, we could feel the energies coming to the surface. When that happens I know we are about to win, for once they come into full consciousness for me and my client, we can use our intention and will to let them go. We released the curse. Here is her account of the session.

The main thing I remember was the immense feeling of love and safety that Anne emanated. She told me that I was carrying a very powerful curse, one that I had carried through every lifetime since it was put on me in a life in Egypt.

Anne said the effect of this curse was to create a feeling of fear and anxiety, a fear of abandonment and rejection, a life of hardship and struggle, physical abuse (Anne knew nothing of the abuse and two rapes which happened in my twenties), ill health, financial difficulties, scarcity and lack. Again Anne knew nothing of the voluntary bankruptcy that I declared in 2005. Everything that Anne said was represented by the curse I had actually lived through in this lifetime. She gently and lovingly removed the curse and told me that I was extremely loved and safe. From that day to this I have felt tremendous love, peace and connection to divine source. In short, the experience with Anne was life transforming and I haven't looked back since.

It's easy to become paranoid about curses and blame every bit of perceived bad luck on a curse. In my experience, most of the time our negative experiences are created by our own pessimism, our fears and our sense of separation from our Higher Self and God. But if you do think you have been cursed, then here is a way that you can let it go. Remember that you have free will, and you also have a connection – a very powerful one – to the source of light. Light is always stronger than darkness, positive energies are greater than negative energies, divine love is more powerful than any curse or black magic. Nor are you alone in any battle you may have with dark forces, demons or the negative thoughts of others. You have hosts of angels, battalions of spiritual masters and the full force of God's divine love on your side. Ask for help and it will come – get the good guys working for you!

Releasing and healing curses

Follow this healing as though I am talking to you directly, and say the words you are asked to speak out loud strongly and firmly, with conviction. It's important to speak out loud, for the sound of your voice holds its own healing vibration as it connects to your heart centre. Your words send out to the universe your choices, your own divine power, your intention to heal, your intention to be free, and a recognisable declaration of your free will. You might find it helpful to have a friend read this to you.

✧ Find a quiet place and plenty of time for this session, some-where you can speak out loud without being interrupted.

I surround you with a ball of pink light of love. I surround and seal your room with a blue light that allows only love to enter. You are in a sacred space filled with love, and you are invis-ible to all but love.

✧ Are you ready to release this curse? Are you ready to heal the damage it has done to you? If yes, say it out loud.

We call in your spirit guides and angels to be with you now. We call in Archangel Michael to assist in clearing this curse.

We put out to the universe and to the heart of God your intention to release and let go this negative energy and send it to the light.

Right now we release the energy that is not of love and send it to the light.

✧ Say out loud '*I invoke the right of my free will to release and let go all negative energy that has been placed upon me by another in this or previous lifetimes. I release it right now.'* Repeat another three times, so four times in all.

We call in the healing energies of divine love to fill you and heal you.

✧ Say out loud, *'I am filled with divine love that heals me through mind, body and spirit.'* Repeat three more times.

✧ You are blessed with divine love – I send you my love and blessings too.

Well done! Now take some time to let those energies of love flow through you. I suggest you also repeat the session of connection and integration to your divine self as I did for my client, for it will be more effective now that you are clear of the heavy energy of the curse.

ADDICTIONS

When you yearn for something constantly, you create a stream of energy that flows through your energy field, and because it's disempowering it has a negative effect. It will lower the general vibration of your aura, decrease your resistance in all respects and generally make you feel weak. It will also break a hole through the outer rim of your aura, with challenging results. When your aura is open like this, negative energies from around you can infiltrate. These energies may simply be other people's thought forms, but if your addiction is severe – for example to hard drugs or alcohol – and long lasting, you may also be affected by the spirits of other addicts who have died. If they were severely addicted in their own lifetime they may still be around the earth plane looking for ways to satisfy their needs, and they may latch on to your energy through the rent in your aura. This makes life particularly difficult, as you are then coping not only with your own addictive needs but with those of the spirit who is piggybacking on your energy field.

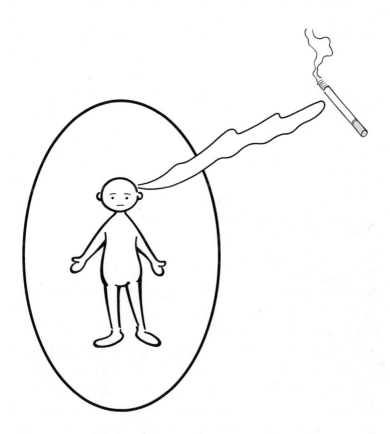

Addiction thought form

WHAT CAN YOU DO?

Once you heal your own addiction, your aura will seal and you will be free of the attention of other spirit addicts. You are the only person who can decide whether your addiction needs serious attention, whether you are prepared to disconnect completely from the object of your desire. No matter whether your addiction is for food, drugs, cigarettes, alcohol or shopping, you will need to release yourself from the attachment in order to release the energy streams that make cords that bind you, that draw your thoughts and emotions towards it. It's your choice, but if you want to feel empowered and strong then you have to make that choice to use your will power over the power of the addictive substance or pattern.

This is a chicken and egg situation. To connect to your greatest power you need to release all these limiting factors, but once you are connected it will be easier to resist. The connection comes in stages, so you may well find that as you work through the contents of this book and the exercises I introduce, it will become easier to release yourself from your addictions.

I know that since I made the connection with my Higher Self, I have certainly found it easier to make and hold my personal choices instead of being bound by old patterns and attachments. I have a love of good food and some not so good food like sugar. Now I have 'found myself' and am able to work with my higher energies, I find it relatively easy to resist chocolate and the wine gums I love. I still enjoy a treat and a drink ('thank goodness', says my husband), but I am now in control of that choice, which is a very empowering state. While you are working towards this stronger position, there are several things you can do.

HEALING THE AFFECTS OF ADDICTION

✧ Cut the cords of attachment (see Chapter 4).

✧ Join a support group such as Alcoholics Anonymous if you crave alcohol, or a slimming club if you are a food addict. It's helpful to be with other people who have the same problem and to get the advice of group leaders who have been through the same experience as you. Giving up drugs is a specialist subject and your local health care expert can help you find support.

✧ Use affirmations that remind you daily of your choice to change: 'I choose what food I eat, I eat healthy and nourishing food', 'I respect my body and decline cigarettes', etc.

✧ See if you can find the cause of the need or addiction. Beneath the craving will be a wound of some sort that drives it. We will be going deeper in the chapters that follow and you may come to understand your trigger as we go along. Make it your intention to seek out the underlying cause. This intention will in itself help you to understand it.

✧ Visualise your energy field and see the holes your addiction has caused start to close. Say 'My aura is strong and I heal all breaks in my boundaries.' Visualise a blue light surrounding the outside. Say 'I am sealing the edges and preventing temptation from coming in and blocking the thoughts of my desire to reach out.'

✧ Your boundaries are always threatened when you are prone to saying yes rather than no. Learn to say no. Repeat to yourself, 'I can say no.'

THE MEDIA

Fears that we pick up from outside – from our culture and from society – can have the effect of pulling us away from our path towards connection. The media are particularly good at drawing our focus to the material world and away from our spiritual aspirations. Society is very good at creating fears, helped along by the media who are looking for sensations and drama in order to sell papers or advertising. This reinforces our own natural tendency to fear the worst – and, of course, we enjoy the drama.

A simple example is the way we allow ourselves to be talked into fearing certain types of food. We have been told to fear shellfish because they create cholesterol which will encourage heart attacks. Potatoes put on pounds of weight, while the green bits in the skin can be poisonous. Bread clogs up the digestive system and will also make you obese. Milk . . . there is no end to the sins of dairy products, including creating mucus. Wine and alcohol will give you a heart attack and ruin your liver . . . Oh, but I forgot, everything has changed now – shellfish is a good source of low fat protein, potatoes are good for fibre if you eat the skins, we should drink milk to give us the calcium to stop the growing danger of osteoporosis, red wine can *prevent* heart attack. Ah, the demons are being laid to rest!

Seriously though, we are easily led down the road to fear. It's up to us as individuals to find out what suits us and to avoid falling into the trap of becoming anxious because of media sensations. We are prone to being affected by the fear generated by a few acts and powerful words that are magnified by media coverage. Just think how powerful a few nameless and faceless men and women have become through being labelled terrorists. The entire Western world has changed its laws, constrained the liberty of its citizens, created chaos and mayhem with security checks at airports and made currency dealing between countries a nightmare. A very few people have created great fear very successfully. They are our modern-day demons.

Avoid other people's fears.

Exercise to release society's fears

When you have been bombarded with bad news, pessimistic views of the future or negative attitudes from the media, allow yourself to cleanse and release the impact on your own energy, emotions and fears. Here is a simple meditation to bring you back to your connection and detach yourself from the world's problems.

✧ Close your eyes. Focus on your breathing and listen to your breath as you breathe in and out slowly four times.

✧ Put your hands on your solar plexus, below your rib cage.

✧ Say to yourself, '*Through my connection to my Higher Self I am in touch with and connected to the greatest source of love. This love flows through me, banishing all fear and all anxiety, and fills me with light. I release all fears and stand strong in my own light of love.*'

Now let's look at one final cause of heavy energy that we can pick up and carry and which can pull us away from our connection.

RESPONSIBILITY AND DEPENDENCY

When I am clearing someone's aura I always check their shoulders and normally find some thick, heavy energy blocks settled there. These usually come from a sense of responsibility and the burdens that we carry in life. These heavy energies of burdens and responsibilities are frequently caused by work and our families. They can come from things we enjoy, but they are nearly always sourced by a sense of 'must do' – a sense of duty.

Very often the people we feel responsible for don't want us to feel like that at all. They would rather be free to make their own way through life, learning their own lessons without knowing that someone else has taken on responsibility for their wellbeing and happiness, success or failure. Taking responsibility for someone else is very disempowering for them. It makes them feel incapable and useless. How would you feel if for everything you do there is someone somewhere who feels that the outcome of your action is their responsibility?

Of course, you may have an invalid parent or child; the burdens then are real and are inevitably a part of your life. However, many responsibilities are merely perceived, so let's get rid of these. It would also be a great idea to let go any sense of duty, for this too can be a huge burden. If you are culturally locked in to a duty, or if there is something you feel obliged to do because you think it would upset someone if you didn't, then try to do it with a happy heart. As I said, energetically these energies sit heavily on our shoulders, so here is a quick-release and symbolic way to clear their effects.

Exercise to release the burden of dependency

Either do this for yourself or get a friend to help you.

✧ With you hands sweep and smooth over your shoulders, bringing your hands down to your elbows, and imagine you are flicking away the heavy energies.

✧ Keep doing this for a few minutes and say '*I am releasing all my burdens . . . I am letting go the responsibilities that are sitting on my shoulders . . . I let go these "stones" of energy that weigh me down. I send love and blessings to all those I help and care for and I no longer let them be a burden to me.*'

ENERGY HOOKS

Do you carry people on your back? Is anyone depending on you? Are there a number of people who rely on your vitality, your help and your strength? If so you may find that you have energy hooks on your back. These are created by the constant thoughts of the people who depend on you. And because, as we know, thoughts are energy, their constant thoughts of dependency create permanent energy links that terminate in hooks. Although these energy cords supply them with energy, they drain *you*. So it's helpful to release these too.

Exercise to release energy hooks

Again, either do this for yourself if you can, or better still, get a friend to do it with you.

✧ Sweep and brush hands over your back.

✧ Say '*I release all hooks and attachments from the dependency of others.*' You can name these dependents if you know who they are. If they are clients, students or those you help, then say '*I let you all go with love, be strong and empowered in your own right.*'

✧ When you next shower, use a lime or lemon shower gel or rub fresh limes or lemons on your shoulders and back. This will help to clear any heavy or negative energies. You will find it very refreshing – I use it a lot, especially when I have been working.

LIFTING YOUR ENERGIES

Finally, let's see how you can lift your overall energy levels. As I've explained, fear, anger, guilt and other negatively charged thoughts and emotions can make your energy heavy and slow. On the other hand you have recourse to an abundance of energy that can uplift, inspire, bring joy and make you feel really, really good. This is the infinite supply of divine love that you can tap into at any time. When you reach your goal of integration you will eventually be connected to this through your own divine energy source, your monad. But in the meantime you can always tap into divine love, call it in, ask for help, pray for the energies of love, compassion and peace. Here is a simple way in which you can call in this energy to help you clear and uplift yourself.

Exercise to raise energies

✧ Find a quiet space. Make yourself comfortable.

✧ See yourself surrounded by a pink ball of light, of love. Around the room you are in is a blue ball of light, allowing only love to enter.

✧ Put out your intentions to clear your energy. See all your negative feelings, all your unwanted cravings and desires leaving you like a dark stream. Let it keep flowing until all the darkness goes.

✧ See a door opening and see light streaming in, bringing love to fill you and your aura. If you struggle to visualise, then just know that all this is happening.

✧ Stay quietly in this space for a while and allow the energies to gently calm, relax and heal you.

So you are now taking control of the energies that affect you on a daily basis, either from your thoughts or from others. Next we can go deeper and find some of the hidden, underlying causes of your separation from who you truly are. We will start with guilt.

Remember who you are - a being of great wisdom, earned through many lifetimes.

SIX

Clearing Guilt and Karma

*With your head bowed you cannot look up and see your
own beauty, love and sacredness.
Feelings of guilt and associated unworthiness keep you
from the presence of your divine self.*

In this chapter I will be focusing on guilt, which is the
greatest saboteur of inner peace, the strongest prohibitor of
self-love. It is the most powerful barrier between you and
your acceptance of divine love, the essence of who you truly
are, your divine self and its full power. It's essential to heal
all guilt and karma, as it prevents you from integrating with
the energies of love that you hold in your Higher Self. While
you feel guilty you will not be able to reconnect.

Guilt sends out messages to you and the world that say I
AM NOT WORTHY. I am not worthy of love, I am not
worthy of success, I am not worthy to call myself divine, I
am not worthy of my full power, I am not worthy to have
God within, I am not worthy of happiness, I am not worthy
of inner peace. If you are to allow full integration of your

monad's energies of pure love, if you are to allow yourself access to your divine powers, if you are to allow yourself to grow and evolve into being the greatest you can be, you have to release any guilt you hold.

Karma and guilt are closely linked. So I'll look first at what karma is and its effect on our lives, its relationship with guilt and what you can do to release it.

KARMA

Karma is a spiritual law. Spiritual laws are spiritual truths – in other words it is not up for discussion as to whether they work or not. They just do! Karma is the law of cause and effect. If you do something – anything – you will get a return of energy, a consequence to your action. If you do something good like a loving, kind or compassionate act, love will be returned to you. This is a universal law that touches everything created on Earth and throughout the galaxies, so the returning love is not limited to your nearest and dearest or the receiver of your kindness.

If you are helping the old lady next door with her washing and shopping she may or may not appreciate and return your kindness, but at some time you will get love back, often when you least expect it. For this is not a law of expectation. You cannot determine the way it will work for you. You cannot insist that the man you love will love you back, for example – sorry, girls! By the way, love needs to be unconditional – without strings – if you want it to return. If you do the old lady's shopping with the intention of picking up Brownie points and karmic credits you are less likely to succeed. If you help her because you feel sympathy for her immobility and want to be of service, then it will work for you.

All service is rewarded. All kindness is noticed by the world of spirit and those that watch over us from the higher realms. Every kind thought and action brings light to our world, and the greater consciousness of all our connected energies will be grateful to you. In the old days we would have said that God rewards those that do his work. Now we see that loving each other, doing charitable and caring acts, is the work of God and that the reward comes from all of us – for collectively we are God.

In terms of energy karma works on the basis that like attracts like. If you are a loving person you will draw other loving people towards you and likewise be drawn to them. If you are holding anger and hate, you will draw towards you other like-minded people.

Your soul knows these truths. It feels the loss of love that comes when you send out energy that is not love, or if you do anything that breaks your integrity. Your integrity is your own knowledge of what is right and wrong; of what is done in the name of love and what is not. You can fool others but you can never fool yourself. Your inner essence, which always holds that divine energy of love, will know when you act out of accordance with this truth. In other words, if you do something that hurts others, say something deliberately to upset someone, tell lies, distort the truth for gain or cheat and steal from others, then you will feel this as guilt. If you have separated yourself from your divine spark, your Higher Self, so much that you have lost all connection with your real essence of love, you may not be able to recognise when you lie, when you are doing wrong, when others are suffering, or even care about the feelings of others.

EVIL

When someone is totally in denial of their true essence – in other words when they are as far from being connected to their Higher Self as they can be – they are in the state that we know as evil. They are simply unable to feel or give love – usually due to immense pain or loss of recognition of the divine. This means they can hurt others without feeling guilt. If a child is abused consistently from birth it can lose its sense of feeling as it shuts down. We will address this problem of the deep soul wounds created by abuse in Chapter 7.

There are many stories around that show that such children can still manage to survive and become fully functional adults and loving parents. For example, the book *A Boy Called It* by Dave Pelzer tells the story of a boy terribly traumatised and his journey of healing and learning to love again. On the other hand, there are those who have had great parents and a terrific upbringing yet still move away from love. They hurt their parents, they hurt those that come close to them, they hurt society and anyone that crosses their path. The further they move away from compassion and empathy for others, the more they lose their sense of integrity, their self-esteem and their sense of worth. They then put up even more barriers to love because they don't think they are worthy of it.

In fact I don't believe there are many people who are truly evil, completely disconnected from their feelings or from their connection, but unfortunately those that are can do an awful lot of damage, because they are totally dissociated from the effects of their actions and they don't care.

BELIEF SYSTEMS

Religious extremists who believe that evil acts of terror, abuse of women and the superiority of men are spiritually permissible will have to work through the karma of this, either in their current life or the next. No matter what interpretation is put on spiritual teaching, behind every religion based on the reality of God and the divine is the message of love. Unconditional love is the world's strongest and most powerful energy and will heal and restore you to strength and wellness. As you give out love and kindness, so you receive the elixir that your body, your mind and your emotions desire. Unless you believe in this and work towards it as your spiritual goal, you will collect karma no matter what religion you follow.

Karma can work for or against your wellbeing depending on your actions and approach to yourself, others and life. Let's now see how it works in our daily lives and affects us in the bigger picture of our soul's journey through the cycle of life and death over many lifetimes. We'll look first at small misdemeanours and how they affect us. Afterwards we'll consider major causes of guilt and how we can deal with them.

HOW DOES KARMA AFFECT YOU FROM DAY TO DAY?

With negative karma comes guilt – the lack of self-respect we feel when we have broken our integrity. The converse of this are the positive feelings of self-worth we experience when we have done something loving.

As you evolve, as your vibration speeds up, as you grow lighter, so your sensitivity to right and wrong becomes sharper. This means that the smallest deviation from your truth will affect you. Here are some of the ways in which you may be affected. The intensity of these sensations will be governed by how far from your integrity are your actions or words and the level of your sensitivity.

✧ You may experience butterflies, a jab of pain or an uncomfortable sensation in your solar plexus, below your ribs. This is the site of your energy centre that deals with emotions.

✧ You may feel your throat constrict if you have said something that breaks your integrity. Your throat is the location of the energy centre that manages your communication and expression.

✧ You may blush and feel hot and sweaty.

✧ You may feel cold and a sense of dread.

✧ If what you have done feels really bad, you may have a sensation that runs through your entire body.

HEAVY GUILT

If you have done something seriously wrong – like driving drunk and causing a serious accident, maybe even killing someone – then the sense of guilt will pass right through you and lodge in your soul. The negative charge of the guilt will create a soul wound, and it can take several lifetimes to work through and heal it.

There is nothing I can say to someone who has gone through this to relieve them of their sense of low self-esteem – which is of course their karma, the effect of their act. In a healing situation I may be able to help, as I am able to release karma when the soul and God are ready for it to be released. This is often some time after the event, sometimes lifetimes. It is unlikely that you will be able to shed the karma of killing someone, even accidentally, days after the event unless you have lived your life in the highest spiritual order, for example by serving others with love and compassion. As karma is a spiritual law, the time and permission for release comes from spirit, where the bigger picture of your lives can be seen. I cannot say 'Oh, this is a good person, I will let them off the hook.' True contrition and remorse from deep within your heart can open the way to a clearing of karma. However, the guilt you feel at a conscious level may take longer to let go. Drivers of vehicles that have been in crashes where someone has died often suffer remorse and guilt all their lives.

HOW CAN YOU HEAL AND RELEASE YOUR KARMA?

Forgiveness and service are the antidotes to guilt and karma. For small misdemeanours you can ask forgiveness directly of those you have hurt. You can of course also forgive yourself, for this is the most effective release of guilt – allowing yourself to be forgiven. Then you will be able to regain self-love. You can work on releasing your attachment to the past too. For when you have done something wrong, you tend to keep going back and reliving the moment and feeling it again. To clear karma you need to work through your 'karmic debt'. This is the negative karma you have accumulated through this life and previous lives. For example, you may have received good fortune without giving back either to those who helped you or others, or it can be guilt you hold from hurting other people, or promises you have made that you haven't fulfilled. You can clear this debt by helping others and working for the good of mankind, the environment, animals and so on.

You can also clear karma by going through the same suffering you caused others. If this has been your choice, you will have made it a part of your plan for this life before you came, so you won't be aware of why you are experiencing a tough life. However, you aren't doomed to suffer your entire life, for as soon as you achieve your intention of understanding the suffering of others and have achieved the level of compassion or humility you were aiming for − or have learned whatever lesson you wanted to learn − your suffering can end.

The greatest challenge then is to step out of the pattern of negativity that you have lived. If you have reached the stage that your soul needs to achieve, then the karmic clearing we will shortly be carrying out will set you free. You may find past life regression therapy helpful to discover the cause of any karma. We will be focusing on this in Chapter 7 and I have given the details of an excellent therapist, Janet Thompson, in the Resources section at the back of the book.

Once you have acted inconsiderately you will need to regain your self-esteem. Caring for others will help you restore both this and your sense of self-love. So to relieve your feelings of guilt, to clear your karma and regain your self-love, you need to give love, give help, care for others − in other words you have to give love and assistance when and wherever you can, either to individuals or groups.

I don't see karma as a punishment in any sense, other than that the guilt we hold does in fact punish us. This punishment is not given out by another − or by God. But if you feel guilty, you can draw negative experiences to you through the subliminal messages that you send out − thought forms that say 'I am not a very nice person, I don't like myself, I am beating myself up so you can beat me up and hurt me too.' Sometimes you may need many lifetimes to free yourself of the pain of guilt. During some of these lifetimes you will face many challenges because of the guilt you have deep inside.

You will hear people saying 'I must have done something very bad in a past life to have such an unlucky life this time,' but they often miss the point that they are actually drawing this bad luck to themselves. They are not serving time like a prison sentence. So the more you do to help others and to learn to love yourself, open your heart and give and receive love, the quicker you can release this guilt and feel good again.

MY STORY

I would like to share with you now my own story about guilt, as it may resonate with you and give you hope for getting over this major hurdle.

I approached an excellent channel of spiritual guidance, Claire Montenara, to help me clear the blocks preventing my spiritual progress. She was at that time channelling spiritually evolved guides called the Masters of Light. They took me back to a life in my past where I picked up guilt and karma – big time!

I saw myself as a man in a lifetime that seemed to be in Egypt. I was a seer, a clairvoyant and channel, able to bring in spiritual energies to heal and manifest things. I was discovered by the court of the time; there seemed to be a senate or similar governing group, many of whose eminent members would consult with me. At first I worked with spiritually evolved masters from the higher realms who worked only with love and good intent and all went well. Then one day a couple of the senior members of the senate came to me and asked me to 'fix' an election. They wanted me to make sure that the 'good' candidate won. I agreed to do so, for I sincerely believed that this man was ideal for the position and would make a brilliant leader for our country; I also knew that his opposition was corrupt.

However, when I put the request to my spiritual guides they refused me permission. They told me that to ensure the voters chose our man would be interfering with their free will. This was incompatible with the spiritual law of light and love that they stood for. Apart from believing in the cause, however, I also wanted to please the men who had approached me; my ego would take a huge knock if I had to say that I couldn't do it.

Then I heard a voice saying 'We can help you.' I was being approached by the lords of darkness, who offered to give me the power I needed to sway the minds of the voters. I have to admit I went with them. How bad was that! From that moment I was on a slippery slope, and whenever I was refused the power of light I turned to the dark side. This went on for some time, till eventually I was killed by a friend of mine (she is a friend in this present lifetime too). My friend helped rescue my soul in collusion with the angel of death, who grabbed my soul when I died and led it to the gardens of healing in heaven.

Once I came to in the spiritual realms, I realised the terrible thing I had done. I was mortified and filled with guilt. I had come into that lifetime as a light and shining soul with great gifts and I had abused my role because of ego (can I make the excuse that I was a man in that life-time?). I vowed to return to earth and humanity all the light I had stolen by using the dark energies, and swore to dedicate my lives to helping others until my karma was cleared.

This deep guilt still resided within me even in this present lifetime. But I have worked at letting it go and accepting that my karmic debt is now cleared, as I have completed many lifetimes of service since that time. Since I let the vow and the guilt go I have been able to release the sense of anxiety that I have held since a child, and I have also been able to reconnect to my Higher Self. I am now free to do the work I do not to clear my conscience and follow my vows, but because I want to.

WHAT ARE THE SIGNS OF OLD GUILT?

You will know of any guilt you hold from this lifetime, but how do you know if you are holding old guilt created in a past life, as I was? One of the problems we face when we return to Earth and start a new life is that we do not remember who we were or what we did before. The reason is that it would colour our approach to this life. It's hard enough coping with the memories of difficulties and painful experiences we have faced in this life without being reminded and having constant flashbacks of the traumas of the past. However, the wounds of the past do remain deep in our soul, as does the guilt of the past that we have not resolved. There are certain symptoms of behaviour and attitude, feelings and sensitivities that indicate that you are carrying guilt.

SYMPTOMS OF OLD GUILT

Here are some clues that might guide you to the realisation that you are holding on to old guilt:

✧ Ever since you were a child you have suffered with low self-esteem and have always thought badly of yourself. Because this attracts the same attitude from others, your parents may well have put you down and apparently under-valued you.

✧ You seem to lack confidence no matter what you do or achieve.

✧ Physically you carry more weight than you would wish. It seems almost impossible to lose weight and you yoyo up and down. This is because you use a fat coat to hide yourself from the world.

✧ You spend your entire life trying to please others, as though you are endlessly seeking approval.

✧ You put others first – family members, work colleagues, even strangers. Their comfort and their needs seem to be uppermost in your mind all the time; you even take the blame for situations without reason.

✧ You give so much of yourself to other people, other causes or organisations, either through work or voluntarily, that you sacrifice your own health and wellbeing.

✧ You have difficulty in finding love – either from a partner or from friends or both. If you do find love you seem to sabotage it or let it go easily.

✧ You are followed through life by a constant fear or anxiety about doing something wrong, making a mistake, upsetting other people or breaking a rule.

✧ You have a feeling that you need to justify yourself all the time – your actions and your words.

✧ You feel a sense of fluttering inside – like a mild panic attack – a lot of the time without any apparent reason.

✧ You feel that you have been unlucky all your life and can't understand why – as if life has dealt you a bad hand.

Any or all of these symptoms may be caused by old guilt. I know a lot of mothers, therapists, carers and healers who just give, give and give more without any consideration of their own needs, either emotional or physical, until they burn out and become ill. This sense of self-sacrifice is typical of two karmic situations. Either you have done something that you consider wrong at some time and the guilt drives you to clear it, or you have made a vow to give of yourself as a self-sacrifice. We will look at vows later in this chapter but even they are often made following a need to clear guilt.

If you feel that any of these signs indicate that you need to heal the guilt, the following exercises may help you. It's a great idea to work through them anyway, rather like a spiritual detox.

HEALING GUILT AND RELEASING KARMA

Here are some ways in which you can help yourself to clear away the awful burden of guilt. Your soul will let it go if it feels that the time is right – that you have learnt the lesson and understood how badly being out of your integrity affects you.

Forgiveness

If you have upset someone in this lifetime and they are still alive, ask for their forgiveness and then let go your attachment to the blame. If they are no longer alive, you can follow this short visualisation which will take you to a place in spirit where you can connect to their spirit. This will allow you to see them as you remember them best.

✧ In a quiet place, sit comfortably. Close your eyes. Breathe in and out deeply to the count of three for each breath.

✧ See yourself in a beautiful garden, a place of healing, peaceful and serene. Sit on a bench and see the person you wish to contact come through the mist towards you.

✧ Let them know that you wish to be forgiven and allow them to forgive you.

✧ See this as a true letting go of that old guilt and allow yourself to be free.

Try to forgive yourself. See that the guilt you carry is a burden that you alone can let go. Make the intention that you will let it go, for it is holding you back in your journey to peace. It is a barrier to your reconnection to your higher powers.

Service

Helping other people, animals or the planet will help you rebuild your self-esteem and allow the burden of guilt to be lifted. But please, please do not do this with the aim of sacrificing yourself. It is not necessary and the rule is to love yourself as well as others. Any other way will slow you down. Keep in mind the intention of caring for yourself as well as your family, friends, causes, etc. Once you burn yourself out you are no good to anyone, for you will then have an illness to cope with as well! However, kindness, time and the act of giving without reward is karmically powerful. It will release your soul from the burden of guilt and allow you to regain self-respect and self-love.

The act of giving, of service, of offering love and
compassion, gives more to the giver than to the receiver.
It will allow you to bloom and glow and is a potent
method of healing yourself at the very deepest level.

Exercise to release guilt

When I work with someone I can often feel their pain and
see its cause – both the pain they feel now and what they
felt at the time it first occurred. This helps me to find the root
cause and then we can heal and release it together. I will now
take you through the healing I give in these sessions. As you
read this, imagine that I am speaking to you directly and with
your permission I will clear away the old guilt, as you release
your attachment to the old energy and the karma.

✧ Find a quiet spot to do this exercise and allow some time.

✧ First you need to hold the intention and the conviction
   that you are ready to let your guilt go. With your free will
   and the ability to choose, you can say out loud that you
   are ready to let all guilt be forgiven and released. Please
   do this now . . . Say 'With permission from my soul, I release
   and let go all guilt, I forgive myself and am forgiven.'

   I assert my intention of helping you release the old pain. With
   divine grace, love and forgiveness, your karma can now be released.

   It is now cleared and with love and forgiveness it leaves you
   right now. It leaves you as a dark stream that flows away to
   the light, where it dissolves and becomes your strength and
   wisdom. Know that everything that ever happens gives you
   strength and understanding.

   Allow the heavy energy of guilt to leave you now.

◈ Take your time before you return to the room.

Bless you.

IS IT POSSIBLE TO BE FORGIVEN OF ANYTHING?

Yes, even murder. For we have all done unloving, thought-less or cruel acts in our time. Otherwise we would never learn what is love and what is not, what is good and what is bad for us; what hurts and what doesn't. We learn the differ-ence between light and dark, good and bad, love and hate while we are on Earth. Unless we have the full knowledge of being both the giver and the receiver of traumatic, cruel and unloving experiences, we cannot discern or learn about love and lack of love. So everything can be forgiven.

Remember too that cruel acts are normally the result of inner pain. Only people who are hurting inside, who are separated from their own love, other people's love and divine love, will deliberately lash out and hurt someone without conscience. You can't imagine the Dalai Lama or Nelson Mandela deliberately speaking cruelly or hurtfully or stabbing someone – can you? People who are evolved, who have healed their wounds and are in touch with their Higher Self and God/Source, just don't do those things. They have no reason to do such things – no pain to transfer to others, no anger to put out to the world. They have healed it all.

So, in summary, karma and guilt change our energy, lower our self-respect and wound us. The messages we send out to the world draw towards us a form of retaliation; we become magnets to situations and people that will bring towards us negativity matching the negativity we have created with our actions and words. We hold this guilt as discomfort and inner pain until we can re-establish our self-esteem. This we can do by loving and compassionate actions and words. Then, by learning our lesson and forgiving ourselves, we can let our karma go and release the self-inflicted scourge of long-term guilt.

We cannot leave the subject of karma, though, without looking at the limiting and binding effect of vows.

VOWS

In my work I have found that vows and oaths, promises and commitments made either in this lifetime or in the past, can hold you back and limit your life in extraordinary ways. Each one of us has at least twelve unresolved vows at any time. Let me explain how this works.

When you make a promise that has particular significance to you, it comes with the endorsement of your heart and soul. When you make such a commitment from your very core, from your soul, then you will be bound to this vow until such time as you choose to release yourself from it. Vows, oaths, soul contracts are often accompanied by a ritual to show the intensity and sincerity with which you make the promise, the importance that you give to it. In other words, you are intending to follow it and never deviate from it. Some typical rituals and vows you may have made in the past include:

✧ Marriage vows made in churches or during religious ceremonies; promises to stay faithful to your partner, to honour
and obey, to be bound to that person for the rest of your
life.

✧ Spiritual vows made through religious ceremonies.

✧ Oaths made at times of trauma and great grief, for example
'I will never have another baby', after a particularly difficult birth or the loss of a child.

✧ Commitments made to causes, for example 'I give my life
to fighting for freedom' – these promises may have seemed
appropriate when you were a slave, but not so when you
want to be an accountant and have two children and a
marriage in the suburbs.

✧ Oaths of revenge, such as 'I will never rest until I make
you suffer for that'.

These vows are made from heart and soul and are therefore
spiritually binding. Your integrity, honour and self-respect are
bound to the importance of following and observing them
totally, from the moment that you made your commitment.
Many religious and spiritually motivated vows are made 'in
the name of God', which makes them even more binding
to you in terms of spiritual honour and respect. If you break
a promise, especially one that was made in the name of God
or witnessed by God, you will feel the guilt of being out of
your integrity – you will feel shame at a very deep level.
You may have made some of these vows in previous lifetimes; and you may well still be bound by them.

As you can see, redundant vows and promises can create
lasting karmic ties with drastic effects on your current lifetime. We'll look more closely now at these different types of

commitments. We shall see how you can release them, whether they were made in this lifetime or in a past life. Let's start with the vows and promises you make in the name of love.

MARRIAGE VOWS

You will notice that marriage vows made in most Protestant churches have as a terminating clause 'As long as you both shall live', so these will not bind you from lifetime to lifetime. But you may well have made a promise to someone at some time to love them and be with them for ever and ever! That may have been fine for that lifetime, but it's not really a suitable contract for future lives. Such a promise could result in you being locked into a relationship with someone you find attractive or feel drawn to, but for whom you don't feel the intensity of love that would normally lead you to make a lifetime commitment. You may find yourself feeling compelled to marry such a person simply because of your past life vow. In this present lifetime your partner may not have the appealing character and personality that pulled you together last time, and you may find it very difficult to share your life with this 'new' partner.

Such partnerships often end in tears, because you get the feeling you can't live either with them or without the person concerned. Once you clear the vow you will at least be free to leave, if that is your wish, without the deep feeling of compulsion to be together or the subconscious guilt that comes from breaking the vow.

To clear marriage or lifetime commitment

When we get married – no matter what culture we are from – we do it in style. Months of preparation followed by a grand ceremony, lots of friends and family to witness it and

often a huge debt as well! There is no similar ritual or ceremony when we separate and divorce. If you still have vows
of commitment to someone you are no longer with, I suggest
you create your own releasing ceremony. Ask a few close
friends to witness it and dissolve your marriage vows with
love. This will release you from your past love and will allow
you and your partner to be released from your old commitments. As you dissolve the vows, the cords that these create
will also be cut and you will be released from their energetic and spiritual binding:

✧ Have witnesses who support and love you.

✧ Say out loud words like 'With love and blessings I release
myself and [your partner's name] from our vows of
commitment to each other.' Say this three times for full
effect.

✧ Celebrate your freedom in the most appropriate way!

✧ To ensure that you are free of old commitments, clear
any vows that you have made in the past. Say 'I release
with love and blessings, all attachments and commitments
I have made in my past that no longer serve me or [the
other person's name].' Repeat twice more.

SPIRITUAL VOWS

Spiritual vows made in religious fervour during past lifetimes can also haunt you. At the very time of your conception
as a soul, you made a commitment to God, promising to
follow the light at all times, to hold love as the focus of all
your experiences, to follow your divine plan and to return
to God. If you have followed any religious or spiritual beliefs

in previous lives you will most likely have reconfirmed those initial vows through baptisms, bar mitzvahs, wise women ceremonies, confirmations or other spiritual commitments from different cultures. No problems there. But if you have been a devotee, a nun, a monk, a priest or a disciple of a sect or spiritual following that requires obedience and the surrender of worldly lifestyle, you may have taken further vows. These vows may be holding you to a way of life whose rigid rules are out of line with the way you wish to live your life this time around.

Let me tell you about the interesting case of a friend of mine, a student at one of my healing seminars. All her life she struggled to communicate her feelings, while she was also reluctant to speak in public. She attended an intensive healing week in Greece that took place in a centre near a temple of Artemis. We held a ceremony for the autumn equinox at the ruins of the temple, giving thanks to Mother Earth for the bounties of the harvest and all the good things that we had in our lives.

The next day we focused on healing and letting go past imprints and vows. When we cleared the old vows that were no longer helping us, she started to cough and released a huge stream of negative energy. I saw her, in my mind's eye, at a temple many lifetimes ago, taking part in an initiation ceremony to join a spiritual sect. She was taking a vow of silence. She was reluctant to join the sect and I sensed that she was being indoctrinated against her will.

For some weeks afterwards she suffered throat and ear infections as the old energy worked its way out through her physical body. However, she didn't mind the discomfort, because almost immediately things changed for her. She received a number of invitations to give talks about her healing modality. She performed brilliantly at these, while a regular event that she had started took off, gaining large audiences. For some time she still had a slight restriction in her throat before she gave her talks, but fortunately it always cleared as she was about to speak. So this demonstrated the successful release of a vow created in a sacred ceremony.

Here are some other circumstances in which spiritually binding vows may be having negative effects on you in your present life:

Vows that you may still hold	Possible effects in your life now
Vows made as a monk or nun to eschew sex, marriage and co-habitation.	Difficulties with sex, finding and keeping a partner. Seems to be something preventing you from getting close to a man/woman. Nervousness when with the opposite sex.
Vows made as a temple priestess to keep your virginity.	If you are a woman in this lifetime you may have difficulty getting close to a man.
Vows made as a spiritual devotee to give up all worldly possessions and avoid all dealings with money. Vows of poverty.	Problems either attracting financial stability or preventing money from running through your fingers. No sense of abundance in your life.

A young woman who attended one of my seminars burst into tears when I mentioned the problems of old vows. As I focused on her, I saw her in her past life as a monk holding out her begging bowl. She had made a vow of both chastity and poverty in that lifetime. In this life she had problems with sex in her marriage – she was shy and felt awkward with her husband – and neither she nor her husband could earn, accumulate or hold money. We cleared the vow and although I don't know what her sex life is now like (a tricky question to raise!), I know that she has a new husband and seems to be far more prosperous than before.

Clearing spiritual vows

Of course, you don't want to release yourself from promises that are to your advantage, nor do you want to break a commitment to bring light to the world, to help others or the environment. However, it would be to your advantage to release yourself from old and redundant oaths, commitments and promises made to gods, goddesses or other deities that you no longer worship. And why not escape the bonds of poverty, chastity and destitution imposed by old vows, whether you remember making them or not! Here is a simple and effective way for you to bring into play your free will, choosing which vows you want to keep and which you want to let go based on the highest good for your well-being, both spiritual and physical.

Exercise to clear spiritual vows

✧ Find a quiet place. Sit comfortably.

✧ Visualise yourself surrounded by divine light. Say '*I am surrounded and protected by white light and love.*'

✧ Say '*With love I let go and dissolve any vows, made in the name of spirit, that no longer serve my highest good, my journey to love, and that block my reunion and integration with my highest self and the divine.*' Say this three times.

Because we easily slip back into old habits and thought processes, it would be good to do this for seven consecutive days to reinforce your intention.

VOWS MADE AFTER TRAUMA OR GRIEF

We often make strong and emphatic statements of intention when we have gone through a period of great suffering. When healing, either in a group or individually, I gain insights into the blocks that can prevent a person from fulfilling a dream and I often come across trauma-induced vows. I call these the 'I will never . . .' vows. For they are usually a fervent wish and intention never to follow a similar course of action again – usually because it has brought great pain and suffering.

One such vow that comes up time after time – 'I will never, ever give birth again' – can cause infertility. It is often made following a difficult and painful birthing experience or even the loss of a child, which is the most painful experience a parent can endure. One of my clients was a young woman who had been trying for a child for some time. During one of our healing sessions I saw her, in my mind's eye, dressed in a long brown dress and poke bonnet, obviously from some time a couple of hundred years ago. In the first image I saw she stood beside a child's fresh grave, with a number of other small graves next to it. Then I saw her crying, leaning against a fireplace, staring into the fire and saying 'I will never have a child again.' She had obviously lost all her children to some awful illness, and the loss and pain was so great that she could not contemplate ever going through that desperate pain again. After we cleared this vow, my client was pregnant within two months.

Another common vow is 'I will never love again'. Often made after the particularly hurtful loss of a loved one, either through the breakup of a relationship or through death, this can cause your heart to close. Naturally it will prevent you from creating a loving and close relationship. You may have made a similar declaration in your present lifetime!

You may also have made a vow that affects your work. I personally made a vow never again to be highly visible as a spiritual teacher after a lifetime in which I was persecuted and brought to a sham trial. My supporters were fed a lot of lies about me and my work and many deserted me. I felt totally betrayed and decided then and there that I although I would continue to work, I would keep a low profile. This vow held me back in my present lifetime until I was able to clear it. From that moment things changed and I became more 'successful' in terms of recognition and the ease with which I filled seminars and events.

Many healers, carers and therapists I know have been physically abused in past lives by the authorities and many have made vows never to do this work again for fear of a repeat of the past so if you are finding it difficult to get clients or support yourself with your work then you too may need to clear the past. If you are in any form of business and, for no logical reason, are having problems making it successful, you may have made a vow never to become successful following a past life experience where success brought you jealousy, loss of friends or even persecution.

JANE'S STORY

When a vow is cleared, the repercussions can be much greater than we are able to visualise. Jane's story demonstrates this. She called me for help in clearing her grief at losing a baby which had been stillborn some three years before. She was desperate to get pregnant again, but I thought the loss of her baby was acting as a block to her current fertility. She also complained of a constant pull in her stomach – a sense of anxiety that was with her all the time. When I connected with her energy I felt the presence of an old vow that was stopping her conceiving and giving birth – a vow most likely made after a difficult birth in a past life, once again something like 'I will never have another child'. When I cleared the vow, this is what she experienced:

> As Anne started to do the healing I felt that I was taken over by this beautiful energy of colour. I became transfixed by a spiral of what at first looked like cloth but what I then realised was particles of purple and magenta energy. It formed a vortex that emerged from me and spiralled off into the distance, slowly at first then getting faster and faster. Eventually it slowed down, then started to spiral back towards me. When it stopped my vision was filled with magenta colour. I then felt that I was lifted up by cords from my pectoral muscles, underneath my collar bones, which were tender for the next three days.
>
> When I came round I had a sensation in my solar plexus and the knot was virtually gone, taking away the anxiety that I had felt for so long. I felt completely calm and still do – the anxiety has never come back.

Jane had cleared both the vow from her past and her sense of the loss of her child, which had left her with constant anxiety. Even more exciting is the fact that within two months she became pregnant. As I write this book she is expecting her baby in four months' time.

CLEARING PRONOUNCEMENTS FROM PAST LIVES

It is unlikely that you will remember what you have said in past lives, so you will have to base your premise of being bound by old pronouncements on the symptoms you experience in the present. If you feel blocked in pursuit of your goals, there is a good chance that karmic vows somewhere in your past are affecting you. In any case, it's a good idea to confirm your own positive intentions about your work, relationships and your spiritual journey. Here is a way to dissolve your past commitments and reconfirm your present intentions:

Exercise to clear pronouncements from past lives

✧ Make yourself comfortable in a quiet and peaceful setting.

✧ Focus on the areas of your life that are not going as well as you would wish.

✧ Say three times '*I release all vows and commitments ever made that no longer support my highest good.*'

✧ Again say three times '*I am free to pursue my relationships, my work and my leisure activities with total freedom. My Higher Self guides me. I am divinely blessed as everything in my life is filled and governed by unconditional love.*'

COMMITMENTS TO CAUSES

You may have felt so passionate about a cause in the past that you offered your life for its advancement. Such commitments are often prefixed by 'I give my life to . . .' However, I doubt whether you want to give your life right now to the Republican army of the Spanish Civil War or the suffragette movement!

I suggest you release yourself from these redundant causes now:

✧ Close your eyes and put your hand on your heart.

✧ Say three times 'I release myself herewith from all commitments of time, health, life and service to any cause not
   currently in my life.'

NEGATIVE OATHS

In times gone by it was quite normal to curse an adversary.
I once did a clearing in the City of London where we
released a number of spirits caught in the Earth plane by
the curse 'May your soul rot in hell', which terrified them
so much that they were unable to move to the light. Curses,
although maybe not that particular one, are still used today.

Of course, if you were to curse someone there would be
negative implications for your own energy and your karma.
You would hold this negative energy for a long time and
you would owe a karmic debt to the person affected by your
curse. Thoughts and vows of revenge can bring down entire
families and clans, both physically and spiritually. We will be
looking at this in more detail in the next chapter when we
see the effects of the genetic stream of energy that flows
through our ancestors and on to our children. Again, you
may not have cursed anyone, either in this life or before, but
while you are carrying out your spiritual detox it might be
helpful to include this release as well!

Exercise to release negative oaths

✧ Sit quietly.

✧ Say the following healing invocations three times with serious intention: '*I ask forgiveness of anyone I ever caused harm through my words and actions. I rescind and dissolve any curse, oath or negative intention I have placed on any living thing in the journey of my soul.*'

So that about wraps up this chapter on karma, guilt and the karmic ties that are created by vows and curses. Releasing karma – your own and that of others – is an act of love and a gift. Through forgiveness we set ourselves and others free. Each act of healing you do for yourself brings you closer and closer to your goal of reunification and integration with the energies of love and compassion that flow through your higher monadic self.

Well done for the work you have completed so far. I will now take you through ways in which you can release the impact of the attitudes, actions and disharmony behind the genetically inherited problems you may be facing.

Remember who you are - a being created from the source of Joy.

SEVEN

Healing Soul Wounds

Like a balloon held to Earth by a weight, wounds and pain in your soul prevent it soaring high and joining its divine partner - your Higher Self.

In my work as a healer I focus on the soul because many of the problems we find difficult to heal for ourselves are caused by deep-rooted wounds and scars of the soul. They are the unseen and underlying cause of much of our fear, anger and guilt. These hidden scars are also the cause of much of the sickness and disease that affects our mental, emotional and physical bodies. So if I want to clear and release these current problems I need to go back to the source; I need to follow the energy stream that connects your pain to the problem that created the wounding in the past.

I am holding this intention when I open up to the energy of a client. As we talk about the problem, if the time is right and the soul is ready to release the wound, the energy charge comes to the surface of the client's energy field. I can then sense it. If it has an emotional charge or a physical manifestation, I can also feel it in myself. I can feel the anxiety which bubbles in the solar plexus, the terror that stabs like a knife, the restriction around the throat, indicating a fear of speaking about feelings, the pain of heartbreak in the heart. Once I can feel the problem and connect to its energy stream, I can follow it back. I often get a glimpse of a past situation, either from this lifetime or a previous life, which appears to me like a short video clip. Then, together with my client, we can release the imprint, the energy charge that the past trauma has left on the energy of the soul.

I should emphasise here that all releasing, all clearing, all healing is done by you, not by me or any other outside force. I am merely the facilitator of your healing. I give the love and hopefully the understanding that opens you to your own healing. All decisions about your wellbeing come from *your* Higher Self.

In this chapter my intention is to take you through the causes of soul wounds so that you can consciously acknowledge and understand the root cause of your problem. I will help you look at the emotional and physical symptoms that give clues to what may lie underneath. When you read those that relate to your problem you may get a frisson or energy 'shiver'. This will be your subconscious accepting and acknowledging the experience that created your condition. The feeling will be different for everyone. It may simply be a deep knowing, or it may be a physical sensation – an ice-cold shiver that runs through you, or a wobble in your tummy, or a feeling of heat, or a physical reaction like a stabbing pain as your etheric body remembers the situation and the pain of the original trauma.

CURRENT LIFE COPIES OF PREVIOUS LIFE TRAUMA

You may have created a situation in this lifetime similar to the one that caused your old wound. This will bring your focus to the need for healing, and as you heal the scar from this lifetime the underlying wound will also heal. It may not be as profound or devastating as the past experience but it will draw your attention and healing. However, if you have attempted to heal this wound in previous lifetimes without success you will have a deeper and more impressionable experience in your present life. It will continue like a pattern, lifetime after lifetime, until you heal and move on.

For example, I have had to learn a lesson to find a balance in my life between my work and my family. For many life-times I dedicated myself to my work and did not have a partner. This was because a long time ago I had a very painful life in the course of which my husband left me because of my work − I didn't give him enough attention and I lost him. I promised myself not to be in that situation again and from that moment dedicated myself to my work, which was healing and spiritual teaching. My first reaction − one I carried for a number of lives − was to blame my work for this loss of love in my life. This meant I lived my lives alone, without the comfort of a loving partner. It took till my present life to realise that I could have both, but that I needed to manage my time and my affections.

Fortunately, I chose (and this was no coincidence, of course) a man who has dedicated a great deal of his time, energy and attention to his own work. This has left me free to develop mine. Now he has retired I have to be a little more careful about how I use my time, but we manage to balance our lives well. Since I broke the pattern of my past I have the best of both worlds.

Any deep scar or wound that you have decided to attempt to heal in this lifetime will come to the surface at some time. Normally we don't aim to heal everything in one life and you will only have to face what you think you can manage. You will also have made plans to meet others who can help you to face the problem, to highlight it through the way they treat you, and to help you to heal. You have probably already met 'the right person at the right time' at least once in your life. When we are ready to let go an old energy charge that is affecting us through mind, body and soul, then the circumstances are arranged so that we can have help. The very fact that you are reading this book proves to me that you are ready to make this step, ready to heal and release your past, ready to acknowledge who you truly are, ready to claim your spiritual powers.

WHAT CAUSES SOUL WOUNDS?

It takes a very painful experience to wound your soul. A slap from your father or a failure at A level will not affect your soul. Either of these may shame you or cause you tears, but they are not so severe as to go deep into your soul – unless perhaps your exam failure prevents you from reaching your life's dream, a dream you have held every day of your life. Generally speaking, though, you heal hurtful situations like those in just a short time. So what would hurt you so deeply that it caused you to carry an imprint from lifetime to lifetime, disturbing you with fears and phobias that seem to have no cause and initiating reactions that you cannot understand?

Apart from your own emotional reactions which may mystify you, other people may react to you and affect you in ways that you cannot fathom. Remember that your pain and scars send out subliminal messages which cause a reactive response from those around you. For example, if you have been betrayed and hurt by someone in your past whom you completely trusted, you may now hold a fear of being emotionally close and open to people. To prevent someone coming close again and to protect you from the hurt that you now perceive comes with a close relationship, you will have created a shield and wall around yourself. If your past experience also caused you great anger or abhorrence, you may still hold that anger. This can make your energy spiky, almost aggressive. People will feel this and they will keep away, leaving you with an 'issue of loneliness', or with difficulty in creating close relationships.

I will now go through some of the situations I have uncovered during my work and the physical and emotional manifestations that may be affecting you. Afterwards I will show you ways both to heal these old imprints and also to go back to the past in order to discover the cause of your wounds.

BETRAYAL

Betrayal is the most common cause of deep soul wounding that I come across. For if you have ever been harmed by someone you trust and love, then you will hold the sense of betrayal deep in your heart and soul. As betrayal indicates a withdrawal of love, it will damage your heart centre, either breaking your heart or wounding it.

The most profound and deeply wounding sense of betrayal comes at the time of death. Take for instance a situation that I saw in one of my clients. In a previous lifetime she had been male, and was on the battlefield fighting side by side with his family when he was stabbed in the back. As he lay dying he realised that his attacker was his brother, who had turned against him to gain the family inheritance. He had no chance in that lifetime to forgive his brother or to understand what could possibly have driven him to this terrible act, so the wounding carried on to the next life.

I didn't see the intervening lifetimes, but my client

complained that her brother was causing her problems over family matters in her present lifetime. More seriously, she was unable to trust anyone. This lack of trust was stopping her from getting close enough to anyone to love them and have a happy and fulfilling relationship. Once we found the cause, we could let the energy go. I asked her to forgive her brother – who was the same brother as in her previous life – and to let go any bitterness she might still be holding. I felt the energies shift as she went through the process of forgiveness, and we both felt the pain in her heart centre lift. This change in her then affected her relationship with her brother, leaving a clear space between them that had the potential of being filled with love rather than distrust.

Betrayal can manifest in several ways, emotionally and physically. The above case was mainly an emotional one, but I have come across many cases of physical pain caused by treachery. Here are some of the symptoms of betrayal:

✧ Physical pain in the middle of your back.

✧ Pain in your heart centre, which may become more intense when you talk about or focus on trust.

✧ Inability to trust even your closest family.

✧ Difficulty in making a close loving relationship, if you were betrayed by a lover.

✧ A barrier round your heart, which may be closed due to fear of vulnerability.

✧ Fear of death, if you were betrayed at the time of your death.

✧ A feeling of dread and insecurity in a certain place or country; the betrayal may be linked to that certain place or country.

✧ A general sense of insecurity, which can come from loss of trust.

✧ Fearful or anxious feelings, raised because the person who betrayed you may be back in your life.

Healing the wounds of betrayal

You may have vowed to be discerning or, even more likely, never to trust again. If you have issues of trust it will be a good idea to follow this healing process:

✧ To release a vow such as 'I will never trust again', say 'I release the vow disclaiming trust.' Repeat twice more.

✧ Say the following affirmation and mantra daily to reprogramme your conscious and subconscious mind to accept and receive: 'I open my heart to love and I trust with discernment.'

If you have any idea who may have betrayed you, or if you have actually been betrayed by anyone in your present lifetime, you can release the imprint and wound by forgiving them and letting go any bitterness or resentment they may have caused you.

✧ Write down on a piece of paper any feelings of bitterness and anger you feel for the person who betrayed you. Burn the paper. Repeat as often as needed till the feelings have gone.

✧ Close your eyes and imagine you are in a garden or quiet place. Visualise the person who betrayed you in the garden. See yourself releasing the energetic chains that bind you together. Let the person go and if you can, forgive them.

ABANDONMENT

Being abandoned, left alone or deserted is a particular form of betrayal, but it deserves a place of its own as it's one that comes up again and again in my sessions. Many of us have felt abandoned at some time in our lives. One of my clients felt unwanted by her parents from an early age – in fact for as long as she could remember. She couldn't understand why. Although they were not particularly good at demonstrating love, they had never actually thrown her out or rejected her physically. But she felt they could have been far more loving and demonstrative of their affection for her, and she had a sense of being rejected when her sister was born. The sister took all her parents' attention and affection.

This is what probably triggered a vision of a past life in which I saw her as a small girl, left outside the doors of a workhouse in Victorian England. I sensed that her parents had in fact died, but still she felt abandoned by whoever had left her at the gates. I explained what I had seen and it helped her to come to terms with her present life. She explained that her grandmother had died at the time her sister was born and this had a profound effect on her too. So the loss of her grandmother's love, while at the same time the new baby was taking her parents' attention – a common occurrence, small babies do demand a lot of time – combined to bring back the memories of a real abandonment in her past.

There are a number of situations that can give you the feeling of being abandoned, even if it's just your own perception of a situation and maybe wasn't the intention at all.

✧ **Boarding school.** Some children find being sent away to school a great adventure and love it, but others feel that they have been palmed off and aren't loved or wanted any more. A number of my clients have felt they were no longer wanted at home, that they were a nuisance to their parents and had been shunted off to boarding school out of the way.

✧ If **your mother was ill** soon after you were born or when you were small, you may have felt that she was not interested in you. Post-natal depression can come between mother and baby and leave a long-lasting feeling of rejection.

✧ If **your parents divorced**, you may have felt abandoned by the one who left the family home. As women usually have custody, it's easy to feel that your father abandoned you when their marriage ended.

✧ **Rejection by a lover** can break your heart, especially if you are left for another. Whether this affects you at soul level will depend on the circumstances of your relationship, how many other people you have in your life, how long you were together, how close you were and how sensitive you are.

If you are abandoned by a group of people the pain can be even stronger. For example, my aunt's mother left for America when she was young. She took her sons with her and left my aunt with her grandmother. My aunt closed her heart from the shock and the feeling of abandonment went very deep. She was never sent for and she only met her brothers sixty years later when she went looking for them in the States. Consequently she locked down her heart and I never saw her being loving and demonstrative with her daughter. The effects of this scarring were passed on to two more generations, for the daughter then had a strained and difficult relationship with her own daughter – who subsequently abandoned her own children. In this case abandonment not only affected one soul, but became an inherited trait affecting four generations. As a result my aunt also missed out on close relationships with her daughter, her granddaughter and her great-grandchildren.

One of my women clients held a strong sense of abandonment. She told me that it had become a pattern in her life that she had difficulty starting relationships and anyone she got close to eventually left her. When I scanned her to find the root cause, I felt an expectation of being rejected and discarded. It was as if she was sending a subliminal message out to the world: 'I know you will leave me one day.' This in itself either stopped relationships getting off the ground or once established sabotaged them; her lack of trust whittled away the foundations, and her partner would follow her expectations and leave her.

When I looked deeper, I saw her being abandoned at a temple many years ago. She was one of a group of temple priests, priestesses and devotees. The country had been invaded by Gnostic Christians who were defacing and destroying its temples. The group decided to leave and take some of the temple treasures with them to preserve the temple's energy. They needed someone to stay to take care of the temple and their deity (Artemis) and my client was chosen. Her heart broke as the rest of them sailed away and the feeling of being left alone went deep into her soul.

When we healed this past experience, I could feel a great release of the deeply buried bitterness and pain. Through forgiveness of those that left her, both in the past and in her present lifetime, she was able to move forward again with an open heart. She and I are now confident that the old pattern has been broken. Understanding the root cause of the patterns she has experienced in her present lifetime has helped her enormously.

HEALING THE WOUNDS OF ABANDONMENT

You can be left feeling alone, isolated and unwanted by the wounds of abandonment. You may feel unsupported and dread being rejected again. It will knock your confidence and make you reluctant to trust a relationship. It can leave you with feelings of bitterness, anger and resentment. You may find you retire into yourself and are reluctant to mix and mingle.

The one thing you need and the one thing you are rejecting is LOVE.

First, check to see if you are shutting people out before they can get close to you. Like my client, you need to look at the pattern of your life and see if you have shut your heart in your present lifetime due to past experiences. Work on opening your heart (see Chapter 2) – meditate with the intention of seeing the door of your heart centre opening wide. Start by opening up to your friends and sharing confidences. Allow your family to get closer to you – spend time with them individually and alone in order to bond. Check whether you are close and intimate with your own children. Do you hug them? Tell them you love them and give them time and attention. Do you push people away when they put their arms around you, do you shrug them off or stiffen? Hold the intention of bringing love into your daily life simply by giving small signs to everyone you meet. In your mind, know that a smile is a sign of love.

Next, if you have had any experience of being left, rejected or abandoned in your present lifetime, you can do this healing visualisation:

Visualisation to heal abandonment

✦ Find a quiet spot and relax.

✦ Visualise yourself going back to the time when you were rejected or abandoned. Allow the memories to come back to you, even if they're painful and upsetting.

✦ Now see yourself taking this younger version of you in your arms. Hold her/him close to you and calm your fears. Tell this vulnerable and hurting little person that all will heal eventually and that you will grow strong and independent as a result.

✦ Give love and compassion, allowing the tears to flow as you release this old pain and heal it with love.

Thirdly, if you still hold any bitterness towards whoever rejected you, look for ways to forgive them. To help you forgive, get into their shoes and try to understand why they acted the way they did. To help you with this, the following are a few reasons why people 'act badly' towards us:

✦ They themselves were not shown love and affection – just like my cousin's mother and family. If you don't have a role model it is harder to pass on love.

✦ The culturally accepted way of behaving has changed over the last fifty years. A good education was once the greatest gift you could give your child. The boarding school might have been your parents' idea of love. My cousin's grandmother may well have left to find a better life for her children; she may have felt it would upset her daughter to be taken away from her grandmother. It may well have broken her own heart to leave too.

✧ The person who rejected you may well have been unable to trust love themselves. Maybe they felt possessed and controlled, maybe they felt threatened by your love – especially if you were a little desperate. They may have had deep wounds of their own that drew them away from you. See it as their difficulty rather than a personal rejection of you.

Try not to see everyone's behaviour towards you as a test or challenge – you may be focusing on it with a distorted sense of others' negative intent. Perhaps they are going through a bad time themselves and have their own issues to work through. People rarely intend to hurt those they love, but they often do so because of some inability to cope with intimacy or life's many challenges. Avoid taking the role of victim or guilty party. If a relationship doesn't work it's not necessarily anyone's fault; sometimes two personalities just can't work it out together.

Other people have pain too. This can come across as a rejection of you.

ABUSE – PHYSICAL, SEXUAL AND EMOTIONAL

An imprint that can haunt you for a long, long time is abuse inflicted upon you by another, especially when an adult has deliberately harmed you. Most of us have suffered physical injury and harm in one lifetime or another. Life in the past was violent and there have been wars and fighting between families, villages and nations throughout recorded history, so it's unlikely that you have not been affected somewhere along the line. This will not necessarily have caused a soul wounding, but if you experienced violence with cruelty then your soul will have been affected, and if you have been badly abused sexually in any lifetime there will be further repercussions. Here are some symptoms you may experience:

✧ A fear of sex, even with someone you love.

✧ A fear of confrontation. Even violent films on television may affect you adversely, making your heart pound and giving rise to symptoms of fear.

✧ Nightmares and difficulty sleeping. When I was small I had terrible nightmares about being tortured. Eventually I traced these to torture by French collaborators in France where I was helping the Resistance fighters.

✧ Flashbacks and images of violence.

✧ An anxious and nervous disposition – tending to avoid any chance of danger, real or imagined.

✧ Suffering phobias or sickness related to certain places or people. I was always sick when I visited France – this was a direct result of the physical abuse I endured in a past life, which included being beaten in the stomach.

✧ A sense of shame and feeling dirty. This can create side issues of phobic washing and cleaning, and weight problems.

All through Maria's life she had attracted abuse. She felt wretched, separated from the rest of the world. She felt different from other people and her self-esteem was at rock bottom. Yet she was a beautiful woman who on the face of it had a wonderful life. She was successful in her career, enthusiastic to help others and had an extremely loving and caring nature. She first contacted me because she found it impossible to find a relationship and was feeling desperate for love.

As we got to know each other I realised there was a deeper pain within her, and one day she told me her full story. When she was young she was seriously abused by her grandmother, who would pick Maria out for physical and emotional abuse, telling her she was worthless and beating her whenever she could. One day Maria's family went on holiday in the country. She thought this was the best day of her life – she was overflowing with happiness to be in the country, excited to be free to run and play in the fresh air. She came rushing into her house brimming over with joy.

Her grandmother took one look at her and grabbed her. She had dirt on her dress, so her grandmother went into an evil rage and screamed at her. When the owner of the farm came rushing in, she pushed the little girl at him and said, 'She is wicked – take her and do what you want with her.' Being a simple man, he took advantage of the offer. He dragged Maria off into the fields and raped her. This terrible incident left a huge wound, a scar that undermined everything Maria tried to be from that moment on. The pain was embedded in her heart and her soul.

In her healing I found scars beneath this one that went far back, to previous occasions when her grandmother had abused her. She managed to open her heart to receive the love that I channelled to her in her healing. With this love in her heart and soul, she was able to release the imprint from her cellular memory. Instantly we both felt the horrendous pain of this lifetime's suffering leave her. It was like lifting the lid of a box that had been nailed down for a long, long time, and once it was lifted the old energies could be released. Maria now runs a charity that gives advice and help to other victims of abuse. She has managed not only to overcome and heal her past, but to turn it around to help others.

HEALING THE IMPRINTS OF PHYSICAL, SEXUAL AND EMOTIONAL ABUSE

Once you have identified the cause of your problem, you can then focus on your healing. I personally don't think the process used by traditional psychoanalysis of going over old wounds again and again helps too much, especially if you constantly relive the past experience and pain. However, it's important to acknowledge old wounds and the effect they are having on you now. Unfortunately, you are the only person who can let these old pains go; you are the one who can make the decision to let go the past and move on; you are the one who must accept and let go any bitterness you hold against the person who abused you.

However, you can be helped to heal these wounds with love from others. The very first step is to open your heart. Once you are receptive to love then you can go the rest of the way. Like Maria, you need to give your intention to heal high priority. For a long time she boxed her problem away and got on with her life, but sooner or later you have to face the fact that it's impossible to continue your spiritual journey, your growth, your path to total healing while you have these skeletons in your closet. The events that may have traumatised you are shocking – they are deep and hurtful – but they have to be faced. And you have to see yourself in the present – as someone who can renew themselves and shed the scars of the past.

If you think of yourself as a victim, unable to be healed, then you won't heal. But if you see yourself as a survivor, someone who can regenerate and start afresh, then your positive approach will help you to let go and heal. The healing process for imprints that I shall be leading you through at the end of this chapter will help you. I also give healing seminars at which I help people to let go these phantoms of the past and heal the pain, the shame, of the indescribable cruelty of others. You can find details of my healing schedules on my website, which is noted at the end of this book.

PERSECUTION

If you are a therapist, a healer or a spiritual teacher there is a very good chance that you have been persecuted in a previous lifetime. Throughout history anyone who has offered an alternative to the accepted, established and approved religious belief or healing has been seen as a threat to the establishment, the authorities and the church. Even today there is resistance from the establishment in certain countries to alternative healing methods. If you were involved with this work in the past and were persecuted for it, you may now have a deep fear of carrying out your work.

This can manifest in an energy block that prevents you from flourishing and succeeding in your chosen therapy or ministry. When you focus on your work and plan to take it forward, you may bring to the surface and into your consciousness physical memories of the pain of past persecution. One of my clients had very bad headaches, and I had a vision of her in a past life with a length of cloth wrapped tightly around her head in a form of torture. As I looked into it more deeply, I realised that her partner in the present lifetime had also been with her in the past, and as in the present lifetime he had developed a new and powerful healing tool. In the climate of that time it had been too dangerous for him to make this project public and my client became his mouthpiece. She had been captured and tortured in order to make her reveal his secret and his whereabouts. She died by disembowelling, which had left her in her present lifetime with difficulties with her digestive system as well as the imprint of the headaches. She had also been fearful in this present life of going public with her own healing work. She has now cleared these imprints and her therapy work is growing daily. And so far there is no sign of her being disembowelled – even by our health and safety law enforcers!

Until recent times it was quite normal to be martyred for your faith. When religious and spiritual intolerance was rife, anyone who spoke up with new ideas was disposed of, often cruelly. It's amazing how strong people were in the past to stick to their beliefs when they faced dreadful torture. I am so glad we don't have to go through that today! Nowadays we find the self-sacrifice of the old days difficult to identify with. In fact it's quite the opposite – we look to nurture ourselves and make sure that we keep ourselves well and safe. It's important to focus on loving yourself and putting your own health and wellbeing high on your priority list. That way you can be best set up to help others.

So are you suffering from past persecution for your work or beliefs? Here are some of the symptoms that can point in that direction:

✧ You find it difficult to speak about your beliefs – either you choke on your words, or you suffer from a tight or even painful throat. Do you suffer from throat infections?

✧ You blush or marks show on your skin when you get upset, especially in relation to your work or healing.

✧ You feel frightened when you go into a church. This may signify an association of fear with the church and religion. This can apply to temples of any other belief system too.

✧ You suffer pain or a physical problem that has only arisen since you decided to learn a new therapy or become involved with a spiritual practice. One of my clients had terrible pains in her abdomen after she started her therapy training; we cleared an imprint from a wound in her stomach from a past life where she had been a herbalist.

✧ You find it difficult to get started with your own practice, to find clients, to get people to your seminars – even difficulty in starting to teach.

These points do not only apply to you if you are a therapist. Journalists, writers, teachers and scientists can also experience effects on their work that come from their past lives. Anyone who has spoken up for change may have been persecuted, while certain jobs and livelihoods have in themselves been persecuted in the past.

Healing the imprints of persecution

If you think that you have imprints and negative memories of persecution or martyrdom, then you can work with this healing:

✧ Close your eyes and relax. Become aware of your body as you breathe in deeply four times.

✧ Focus on the symptom that you feel indicates a past trauma due to persecution.

✧ Work your way around your body, feeling and looking for any sensations that come up as you focus on the past. If any visuals come up – if you sense anything that is associated with the past – stop and send love and healing to that part of your body.

✧ Now send healing and love to yourself in that lifetime. Feel love and compassion as you embrace and tenderly care for this hurting and suffering person that is trapped in the past.

✧ See a line of dark energy leaving you like a stream – see it becoming light as sunlight strikes it. Know that all your past pain is now turning into your strength and giving you empathy for others suffering for their beliefs today.

We will do more work on past life regression later in this chapter. You may then have a clearer idea of the cause of your problems.

SEPARATION FROM GOD

So far we have been looking at the problem of being separated from your own aspect of God – your divine self or higher self. Beyond and above your own divinity is the greater aspect of the Divine which we call God, or Source or Greater Consciousness. It is a common feeling to have a sense of being deserted by or separated from God, whatever your sense of your God is. When you go through difficult times you may feel that you are abandoned by God. For lifetimes we have been taught by religions that God will look after us, or will punish us if we do wrong. This has left many of us with the sense that we have been abandoned by God or that we are being punished.

The work you have already done to reconnect to your own divinity will help with clearing this separation, but if you have serious doubts about the actual existence of God, focus on the divine and universal energies of love that flow through all of creation and connect us all. The beauty of nature is the best example of the work of God. As you work on your own connection to your divine presence so you will get closer to the Divine – as we have seen, they are inextricably connected and are as one energy that flows through everything – and will start to feel the touch of God. This is not something that I can teach, for it's an experience and a feeling and you will know it once you have felt it. In my next book I shall be sharing some of my experiences and my journey back to a full connection with God, and offering ways in which you can encourage this connection. In the meantime here is a meditation that you can follow.

Divine connection meditation

✧ Close your eyes, drop your shoulders, release your frown and let your body go soft. Breathe deeply for a few moments.

✧ Hold the intention of reuniting yourself to the love that is the energy of the heart of God. Ask yourself to release all barriers that are between you and God.

✧ Visualise the silver cord that flows upwards from your heart centre in the middle of your chest out through the top of your head. See it connecting to your Higher Self. See the light that flows from your divine presence. Feel the love that radiates from this beautiful being which is your personal aspect of God.

✧ See the silver cord that continues up and beyond, and follow it.

✧ You come to an even stronger, brighter and more magnificent light force. Allow yourself to be immersed in the love that radiates from this source. Know that this love is infinite and unconditional – totally accepting you as you are.

✧ Let the light shower over you and surround you. Become at one with it. You are now bathed in divine blessings – enjoy!

Divine love flows through everything - allow yourself to receive it.

VIOLENT DEATH

Another cause of the wounds that we may carry from life-time to lifetime is the trauma of violent death. Most injuries, cruelty and upsetting experiences happen during a life and therefore we have time to heal the wound, or at least to get over the initial shock. But with a sudden, violent death we don't have any time to heal before we pass over to the astral planes of heaven. Although we can do some healing in heaven, the scars on our etheric body (these are emotional scars rather than physical ones, although some people feel the connection) will be there when we return to Earth. For example, if you were strangled you may have problems with your neck and throat, but if you were strangled because you spoke out your truth, or if you were killed by someone you trusted, you would have much deeper and more serious emotional wounds to heal. We will now look at ways in which you can heal these imprints, even though you are unaware of the initial cause of your problem.

Healing the effects of violent death

Most violent death leaves imprints on our cellular memory. The result is a pain or weakness superimposed on our current body. We therefore need to address our body and the associated fear that this death may have left with us. Focus on any part of your body that gives you problems:

✧ Sit comfortably, close your eyes and relax.

✧ Place your hand or hands on the part of you that holds the problem.

✧ Say out loud '*I release with my free will and choice all memories of violent death.*' Repeat three times.

✧ Say '*I fill the fear with love and the love dissolves the fear, right now.*' Repeat three times.

✧ Visualise the pink energy of love flowing from your hands into the affected part of your body.

✧ Now place your hands on your solar plexus where fear sits. Again sense love flowing into the darkest parts of you, filling them with light.

Well done.

HEALING SOUL IMPRINTS

Only when your soul is completely healed can you make the full and constant connection and integration with your Higher Self – otherwise the heavy energy of your wounded soul will keep pulling you back. So it's important to clear all imprints, whether from this lifetime or before.

As I said earlier, we often hold scars from past lives, scars which have not been healed. In your present lifetime you may have experienced pain and trauma that is a totally new experience for your soul and that therefore creates a new wound. However, for souls that have been to Earth many times, the emotional upsets we experience are similar to past experiences. The new scar sits on the old one and as we consciously heal the new scar we are in fact healing a much deeper wound beneath. The current experience may not be so severe as the original trauma, but your attention has been brought to the unresolved issue.

If you could look back over your past lives, you would be able to see patterns whereby you repeatedly face the same challenges lifetime after lifetime, until you resolve and heal the situation. For example, a client of mine was tortured to death in a past life for practising healing as a herbalist and charm maker. Every time she thought about following her dream as a healer or tried to practise healing she had severe pains in her stomach. I saw the past life experience and told her that it wasn't a problem of her present life but a memory held in her cells that flared up when she drew near to the cause of the old pain, rather like a child who flinches near fire after having once been burnt. The pain in her stomach was a safety barrier that she had put there to stop herself getting hurt again. I asked her if she was ready to let go that barrier, to release the cellular memory. She agreed, and together we released the old imprint. Afterwards she went into her work as a healer without any further problem.

Soul wounds often manifest as physical illness. We are often driven to use healing to solve our problems only when all else has failed; when we have been told by doctors that there is no known cure for our ailment or that they don't know what is wrong. It's been my experience that when your soul is ready to heal it will accept the healing and let the scar of the past go. So I propose to lead you through a couple of powerful healing processes that will help you release and heal these old wounds and imprints. As you may not be consciously aware of the cause of your problem, I will start with a past life regression that is designed to take you back to the root and let you see the under-lying cause. Some people respond to past life regression, while others do not so easily float back in time. Please do not worry if you cannot see or experience anything when following this session, for you will sense and see what you need to see. Trust your Higher Self to guide you and show you what you need. You may be directed to the healing you need by lifetime experiences that help you heal deeper wounds.

Past life regression

I suggest that you ask a friend to assist you with this regression. He or she can lead you through the steps and be there for you if you come across something disturbing in your past. Remember this is in the past and you will see it like a video. As with a video, you can stop it at any time and come back into the present. Focus on a problem that you wish to resolve – perhaps a fear or phobia, or an illness that cannot be healed with conventional medicine.

✧ Find a quiet place without phones or interruptions. Make yourself comfortable and relax.

✧ As you close your eyes, hold the intention that you are going to go back to the lifetime that is the source of your current problem. Ask your subconscious to divulge gently the secrets that it holds.

✧ See yourself surrounded by a violet flame that holds your energy safe and strong.

✧ Call your spirit guides and guardian angel to assist you in this healing. Ask them to give you any healing you need as the past comes up and brings its pain.

✧ Imagine you are walking towards a lift door. This lift will take you down to the past.

✧ Step into the lift and choose the bottom floor. The lift will take you down a number of floors. Count down eight floors as the lift descends.

✧ The lift stops. You now leave it and enter a corridor with a number of doors on either side.

✧ Each door represents the doorway into a different past life. Be guided to the doorway that you need. Know that you are entering one of your past lives.

✧ Take note of what you are wearing, what sex you are. Look around you and see what country, era and culture you are in. What are you feeling? Allow yourself time to see and sense your surroundings and the situation you find yourself in. Stay as long as it takes and tell your companion what you are seeing and feeling.

✧ When you are ready to return or go to another life, leave through the exit door.

✧ When you have seen and experienced all you feel you need, return to the lift.

✧ Count up eight floors. Leave the lift and come back into the room. Let your companion give you a hug!

✧ Write down your experience while it is fresh in your mind. You may find that further memories will come back to you if you meditate on the lifetime you have just seen.

HEALING THE PAST HEALS THE PRESENT

As you acknowledge the past experience that is causing your present-day problem you will find that you are naturally healing the past, which in turn releases the imprint of the experience and trauma. As most of our problems are created by the fear and subconscious memory of past trauma, so releasing the imprints of the past frees us from the effects in our present life. Here is another way to clear the past. This method relates to situations that have occurred in your present lifetime but will also take you back to before your birth.

Releasing imprints back to source

This exercise is also best done with a friend – I will give you the words that your friend can say to you to lead you back. If you would rather, you can record these words yourself and play them back to yourself. Leave gaps between each line to allow yourself time to recall and let go your attachment to past traumas.

✦ Relax and close your eyes.

✦ *'I am taking you back through your last two years – releasing and letting go any pain, trauma or negative feelings. Healing energies heal you during these years.'*

✦ Pause

✦ *'I am taking you back now through your adult years. Slowly we go back . . . Think of anything that comes to mind, release any hurt, let go those that hurt you and allow the healing energies of love to fill you at the time of your hurt.'*

✦ Pause

✧ 'Now we go back through your teenage years, releasing and healing the difficult times, the confusion, the painful times. We heal the teenager now.'

✧ Pause

✧ 'We go back through your childhood years, healing and releasing any pain, any fear – filling the child with love, healing the child. Giving the child any love that it didn't get when it needed it most.'

✧ Pause

✧ 'We go back now to when you were a baby. We send love and healing to the baby, releasing any tension that it is picking up from your parents at this time. Hold the baby in loving arms.'

✧ Pause

✧ 'Now we go to the time of your birth, sending love and clearing the shock of arriving in this world, healing and loving you and your mother. Know that you were wanted in this world – not just by your parents but by all those you have loved since you arrived.'

✧ Pause

✧ 'You are now in your mother's womb. We send you love and strength for your impending arrival. We heal any trauma your mother and father are experiencing at this time and which you can feel and sense.'

✧ Pause

✧ 'We are taking you back now to the Inter-life, in the higher realms where you are preparing for your present life. You are surrounded by Elders and Wise Ones who are helping you *make your life choices for this coming lifetime. Remember, you chose how your life would be.'*

✧ Pause

✧ *'We go back now over all your previous lifetimes, releasing all imprints that are affecting you in this present lifetime. We go back and back, healing and releasing.'*

✧ Pause

✧ *'Back and back we go, healing and releasing, till we reach Source. Allow yourself to connect to the energy that created you. I bridge this energy from the time your soul was evolved to the present and bring the divine energies to you now. Spend a few moments allowing this connection.'*

✧ When you are ready, gently come back into the room. Take time to rest and allow the energies to settle.

SOUL FRAGMENTATION

Whenever I do a healing session I include a soul retrieval. This is the recovery of parts of your soul essence and energy that may have been sent away, rejected, frozen in time or lost through major shock or trauma. Really severe trauma, sudden and extreme shock or great suffering can have a major impact on your soul, to such an extent that it can cause a part of your soul energy to fragment. When the pain is so severe, the soul will send the painful part away to enable the rest of your soul to continue to operate. It effectively shuts down part of its operation. The part that is pushed out will hold an aspect of you that is frozen in time.

This means that you can continue but that aspect of you will be missing. As a result your essence will be diminished in some way. For example, if you were abused by your father you may well have lost the aspect of trust, and also those of self-esteem or self-confidence. These aspects will be retarded and held as they were at the time of the abuse. As you grow you will find it difficult to trust, you will have low self-esteem and lack self-assurance.

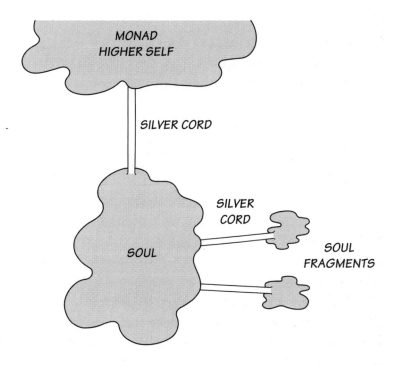

Soul fragmentation

For the sake of the whole, pain that is too intense for the soul to bear is isolated.

But it's possible to recover these fragments and aspects of yourself, because the energy that is isolated and separated from the whole is still connected by a silver cord, similar to the one that links our soul to our physical body and to the full energy of God – our Source. Thanks to these silver cords, when the time is right we can bring back all those parts of us that have been lost in the past.

WHAT CAUSES FRAGMENTATION?

Each one of us handles trauma differently. A lot will depend on how sensitive you are and whether you already had a wounded soul, but here are some of the events I have seen that can cause the soul to be overloaded with pain:

- ✧ **Sexual abuse.** This is the number one reason that I have come across. The shame, the shock and the revulsion can be too much to bear.
- ✧ **Physical attack.** Again the shock and the fear can seriously affect your trust in life and in other people, your belief that you are safe and protected.
- ✧ **Abandonment and rejection** – especially by parents. This can have a huge impact, especially if it came out of the blue or if you thought it was your fault.
- ✧ **Accidents.** Any major accident can shock you into losing a part of yourself. The impact can be enormous, and again you may lose trust in the world to keep you safe, allowing fear to take over. It's not unusual for people to lose their memory without any physical reason after a major accident.
- ✧ **Life threatening illness.** To suddenly lose your health and become disabled in some way, even temporarily, can impact on your soul to the point it that will fragment.

✧ **Loss of a great love.** If a parent dies when you are young and vulnerable it can have a huge effect on your heart and soul.

There are certain times when we are particularly vulnerable to traumatic events, and it is at these times that our soul is most likely to be severely affected:

✧ At **five years old** when you start school. If you haven't mixed a lot with other children before, the change of focus from yourself and your own needs and the necessity to learn social behaviour and think of the needs of others makes this a difficult time. It is also a time of separation from your parents, particularly from your mother. It is a time when any major change or disaster in your family can have shocking results.

✧ At **puberty**, when you are changing from child to adult, emotionally and physically. This is a time when you feel unsure of yourself and you are starting to get to know who you are. If a major trauma affects you at this time you can easily lose part of yourself. It's as if you are loose and unconnected at this time and bits can easily go missing. Once you are sure of yourself and become glued together, then you are more able to withstand the shocks.

✧ For women, at the **menopause** when we leave the age of motherhood and enter that of the grandmother. This is a time when a woman's role often changes and in the transition from one role to another you may well feel vulnerable. It is also a time when you are losing the image of yourself as young and beautiful; in our image-conscious society this can make you susceptible and any loss of love can have disastrous results.

✧ At the **loss of a job or retirement**. Men especially can be hit hard by these events. At such times your sense of self is being revalued and you have to re-establish yourself in your new role. It can be a very trying and difficult time, so if another major trauma occurs you can lose aspects of yourself quite easily.

HOW DO YOU KNOW IF YOU HAVE A FRAGMENTED SOUL?

When your essence is diminished and you don't have access to your full sense of self, life can become a huge battle. Every little hurdle becomes an enormous barrier in your path; you may feel that everyone is against you; the authorities and bureaucracy may seem to be persecuting you. It's easy to fall into the role of victim – things get blown up out of all proportion and your ability to cope and manage your life slips from your grasp.

The effects of fragmentation will be different for everyone and their intensity may vary, but here are some of the symptoms you may be experiencing:

✧ A feeling of not being completely 'here'.
✧ A feeling of being incomplete in some way.
✧ A lack of determination and drive.
✧ A tendency to be easily overwhelmed by life's challenges.
✧ You may suffer from ME (Myalgic Encephalopathy, also known as Chronic Fatigue Syndrome) or other illnesses related to very low energy.
✧ Susceptibility to psychic attack – you just don't have the strength to combat negative forces and energies.
✧ Susceptibility to addiction – you don't have your full determination and will to withstand temptation.
✧ A need for constant support and assistance from others –

you don't feel you can cope on your own.

✧ Difficulty in making decisions – you prevaricate and delay any changes you need to make in your life.

✧ Memory loss with regard to significant parts of your life – the soul finds the memory so difficult to cope with that it shuts it off. Abused victims often forget what happened as an aid to survive the assault.

✧ A deep and abiding sadness that you cannot shift, no matter what you try to do. This is caused by the separation of your soul not only from its own disconnected parts but from your Higher Self and Source – from God.

✧ Loneliness and a feeling of isolation.

✧ A feeling of being 'not of this world', a sense of separation.

You may have lost access to vital aspects of yourself as a result of your fragmentation, and of the wounding that caused it. Let's look now at how your strengths and vitality may be affected.

LOST ASPECTS

As a result of your soul fragmenting, you may have lost touch with aspects of your nature. You may be blocking off and ignoring aspects of yourself, either due to the shock of trauma or following negative experiences and treatment at the hands of others over several years. It may seem that you have locked parts of yourself into a cupboard and that as a result you cannot function fully. Bear in mind here that you put these parts of yourself into the cupboard and you will be able to bring them back out again. This is your healing and you can do it when you feel ready. Here are some of the aspects of yourself that may have become retarded, diminished or held back in your past:

✧ **Self-confidence**. This is one of the first to go as it's our most vulnerable and fragile aspect. It takes very little to crumble the confidence of even the most seemingly self-assured person. If you were in a room with a thousand people and 999 shouted at you that you were wonderful, brilliant and they loved you, while one person at the back whispered 'You're rubbish!', who would you strain to listen to? It's human nature, and hence your confidence will be quick to hide in the cupboard. You can probably trace the day when it first took a battering.

✧ **Self-esteem**. This is very closely connected to confidence but it's the way you value yourself. If you have been abused and rejected you will see this as a reason to lower your own value.

✧ **Your voice.** If you have been severely dominated in this or past lives, you may have lost your ability to speak up for yourself. Lots of people have this aspect in the cupboard.

✧ **Trust**. You lose trust when people treat you badly, whether as the result of a shocking experience that fragmented your soul or through the constant effect of people treating you badly over a period of time.

✧ **Self-love and acceptance**. If other people do not show you love and treat you cruelly and without compassion, then you may have decided to stop loving yourself as well. It's essential that you bring this aspect of yourself out of the cupboard, for you will need to accept yourself completely before your connection and your healing can be completed.

There are others. Do you know what aspects of yourself have suffered abandonment during your life – or which ones in fact you never brought with you? Remember, you can claim them back – so don't despair!

FROZEN IN TIME

Sometimes it's not just a part of you that gets left behind in life's journey. You can actually get stuck at a certain age, a certain time in your past. This means that certain aspects of yourself will have been frozen in time, unable to function fully from that moment, and you will be locked in as you were at that age. Let me give you an example with Jenny's story:

My mother and father were forever arguing. He was domineering and overbearing towards both my mother and myself. He acted in fact as though he simply did not like me; he either ignored me or shouted at me, always telling me that I was no good.

At the age of five my parents split up and my father left, taking my brother. At first it was great, it was so wonderful not being shouted at or ignored, but after a while I started to feel guilty. I thought it was something wrong with me, it was my fault that Dad didn't like me, it was my fault that he it didn't work out with Mum. I felt dreadful because he had totally rejected me. He made no contact with me at all; never called, never visited, didn't send a birthday or Christmas card. He effectively abandoned me. It certainly felt as though I had been abandoned.

From that time my confidence went completely. I thought I was useless and worthless. I found it impossible to speak about what I felt and my throat would seize up, especially if I had to talk in public. I thought that no one would want to listen to me as I wasn't worth listening to!

I worked on my healing for some time and used the The Journey by Brandon Beys to help me understand why my father had treated me like that. I looked back into my father's past and could see that he had not been loved or given any affection in his childhood. This helped me forgive him and accept him. However, my low self-esteem was made worse by sexual abuse that occurred after my father left. This made my confidence even worse.

In my healing session with Anne she said she could see me at the age of five and I was frightened and crying. She sent the little girl healing but said that I had to do this for myself as she was missing my approval and my love. I now spend a few minutes each day visualising myself at that age and giving love to that little girl. As soon as we started this healing the blocks in my ears — which had been there for months, making me practically deaf — cleared, and the tightness in my throat started to ease. I think the ear problem was caused by me shutting out the sound of my father's voice and his disapproval. The throat was because I couldn't say what I felt, there wasn't any point, and anyway my feelings didn't matter or count.

I feel a great weight has now been lifted and I feel heaps better. I can now look at myself in the mirror and like what I see. It's the first time I have ever been able to do this. I can also hear, while I have a job that requires me to speak in public and I don't get anxious at all.

Jenny has healed her soul. She has claimed back who she really is and she is now strong and fully functional in all aspects of her life.

Healing and claiming lost aspects

If you feel that there are aspects of yourself that you may have lost, such as self-esteem, the ability to speak up for yourself, your self-confidence, then use this exercise to help you reclaim your missing aspect. Take a few moments before you start this exercise to focus on the aspect of yourself you feel is not fully in balance or is diminished in any way.

✧ Find a quiet place and relax.

✧ Focus on the aspect of yourself that you feel you have left behind in your life. Think about yourself at the time when this first started to be pushed away or the event that caused it.

✧ Visualise loving and comforting yourself as you were at that time.

✧ Say out loud '*I reclaim my [whatever this aspect is, for example confidence, self-respect, trust]*.' Repeat this three more times.

✧ Visualise this aspect of yourself like an image of you standing strong before you, then stepping into you. Say out loud that you claim this aspect as a strength and a valid part of yourself.

To reconfirm this work and strengthen the anchoring of the energy, create a mantra to repeat every day for two weeks. You will need to make up your own mantra, but here are a few examples:

'I am confident and all aspects of myself are active and strong.'

'I can express my feelings freely and all aspects of myself are active and strong.'

'I can trust with discretion and all aspects of myself are active and strong.'

Soul retrieval

This is the healing I take my clients through to reclaim the energy of all soul fragments that may have been lost in the past. Imagine I am saying these words to you or ask a friend to read this exercise to you.

✧ Find a comfortable and peaceful place to relax.

I surround you with an orb of pink light of love. Your room is surrounded by blue light that only love can enter.

✧ Are you ready to reclaim any soul fragments that may have been sent away in the pain of the past? Answer out loud.

I am sending a love through your heart to heal your heart and soul. The love is unconditional and embraces you exactly as you are. The love flows deeper and deeper into your soul, healing the wounds and filling them with love.

I call back to you now all fragments of your soul sent away in the pain. It is safe for them to return now as you are filled with love.

They return right now like old friends coming home, to make you whole and complete again. They are with you now and you are whole again.

✧ Take time to relax, then gently return to the room.

QUESTION TIME

Can our soul be fragmented when we are born?

We definitely bring soul wounds from one lifetime to another and a fragmented soul is one that is severely wounded. Because you have silver cords holding the isolated parts to the whole, they can be healed at any time in any lifetime.

How do we know when it is time to heal?

Your soul determines when it's ready to let go its pain and to heal. It must feel safe and secure, and your own belief must be able to accept the possibility both of healing and of the need for it. If you do not believe you can be healed you will probably either be in denial that there is anything wrong with you, or will believe that it has to be fixed by a doctor, or that there is nothing that can be done. Once you understand what has caused your problem and you are able to see what can heal it, then you are open and receptive. At that stage your soul can choose to let go the wounding and the imprint of the past.

Can I heal my own soul?

Some wounds you can heal. Through self-love, self-acceptance and all the spiritual work you do on yourself and others you can create the environment for healing. However, there are wounds that are more easily healed by others. It's difficult to channel and connect to the highest vibrations of healing energy and love when you hold sadness and despair in your soul. The sessions I have shared with you in the healing meditation exercises are channelling healing energy to you through my intention and love, so you may well feel the shifts you are looking for. Otherwise you could join a healing group, visit a healer or go on a seminar or retreat. I hold healing events throughout the UK and overseas where I help release negative energies and soul imprints and channel the healing energies of divine love. I can also recommend Brandon Bey's journey work, which takes you back to your past to discover the wounding that you hold.

THE WAY AHEAD

You are now making big steps towards your goal. The work you do on your soul is very, very important as I believe soul wounds are the main cause of many of our emotional, mental and physical problems. All soul wounding, and especially fragmentation, keeps you away from full connection to your divinity. It's essential to heal these wounds and repair your soul in order to enable a full integration with your highest essence, to allow the energy of spirit to flow fully throughout your entire being. Once you have made the first connection and you consciously hold the intention of becoming fully integrated and connected, the energies will start to flow. This in itself will speed up your healing.

Your soul is desperate to heal and the only way it can heal is with love. This love may come from other people, from Source, from your own divine self – but you have to be open and accepting of this, with your mind as well as your heart. As you understand the need for love and acknowledge your own divinity, so the process will start. You will then be moving forward with all aspects of your personality and character in full operation. You will begin to become fully energised, fit, and able to access the power and joy of living as a spiritual being; no longer will your powers be limited to those of a physical being.

Remember who you are – a source of unconditional love.

EIGHT

Accepting Your True Self and Power

When you have healed your wounds your only barrier to complete connection is your own disbelief that you are in fact divine.

Throughout this book we have been working through the connection of your soul's spiritual energy with your monadic energy. You have put your will and intention to do this through the integration process and you have been clearing away the barriers of old pain, guilt and fears that may be preventing the full connection. In this final chapter I will show you how you can focus and allow your mind to embrace the belief that you can truly be divine and allow the connection through belief. Unless you believe something to be possible, to be something that can be available for you personally, then your mind will create its own barriers with beliefs that maybe you don't deserve it or are not capable of achieving it. This will require you to examine your beliefs about yourself and who you are. You need to get through the obstacle of disbelieving that you are divine. Once you have started to make this change and are able to accept that you are divine, you can connect to your divine power. We will look at this power and how it can affect your life. Once you have made the connection, you then need to focus on what you are going to do with this power and the wellspring of love that the connection brings.

You need to allow your mind to accept yourself as you are, otherwise all your doubts about yourself will step up and act as barriers. Every negative thought about yourself and your worthiness acts as a block to your connection with such supreme power. You therefore need to believe that you are OK, that you are perfectly acceptable to spirit as you are, that every part of your being is great – that everyone is a mixture of different strengths and that weaknesses are the balance, allowing the strengths to blossom.

Let me give you an example. I took up flute lessons a few years ago. I proved to be a very average flautist. No, that's a complete exaggeration – I was useless! I enjoyed my lessons but it was a struggle for me. Either I could look upon my venture into the world of music as a complete failure or I could see that my time is better spent writing, teaching, healing, playing golf (I'm not great at that either, but I enjoy it) and, from time to time, painting (again I'm not brilliant at it, but it's better than my flute playing). I play to my strengths and focus on what I *can* do. It's fine to analyse yourself and see what needs to heal – that is really important – but don't confuse identifying wounds that need to be healed with finding fault with yourself.

Knowing yourself is different from judging yourself.

There is enormous power in simply knowing who you are and accepting it – knowing yourself in terms not only of your character strengths but also of your skills, abilities and gifts. However, the most important aspect of yourself that you need to accept and believe is that you are divine. Once you believe this, you become open to divine powers. You have been created from divine energy so you have the powers of the divine. For many of us this is a major stumbling block, for we are reluctant to accept that we can be in touch with such a wonderful aspect of ourselves. It is easier to see fault in yourself than to see the greatness. We tend to see ourselves through a sense of duality – right and wrong, good and bad – which is then reflected into the world and how the world treats us. This creates victims and cause for blame.

To see the best in ourselves and others we need to overcome our reluctance. To help you overcome your reluctance we will look at how you can quieten and still any doubts you continue to hold, opening your heart and mind to believe that you are worthy to accept your divinity. Then you can integrate it fully into your mind, emotions and physicality, letting it radiate into everything you do. Once you accept and integrate fully your Higher Self, where your divinity resides, then you and your work and everything you do will be of infinite power as your energy source is then spirit and divine energy.

Let your ultimate goal be to allow spirit and divine energy to become your energy source and inspiration.

KNOW YOURSELF

So we can see that before you are able to fully accept yourself you need to know yourself. This is comparatively easy, although you need to look beneath the roles you may play in your life in order to see what drives you, pleases you, upsets you and uplifts you. You will need to spend time being self-aware and self-centred while you fathom who you truly are.

SPIRITUAL RETREATS

To help me and to give me quality time focused on myself, I once went to stay for two weeks at a spiritual healing retreat in Brazil – the *casa* of John of God. John is a full trance medium who allows highly evolved spiritual entities to use his body to treat and heal people at a deep spiritual level. In the Resources you will find details of his website and of Phyllis Bennett, a wonderful guide who can take you there and look after you during your stay.

Spiritual retreats are great opportunities for you to find out more about yourself, a chance to go deep within and look for the root causes of your ailments and problems, both emotional and physical. Every year I organise at least one workshop somewhere in Europe, where for a number of days attendees can escape their normal lives and focus on their own inner journey. Information about these can be found on my website. If you want to go to a more exotic location you might like to join a friend of mine, Sandra Gonzales, who works with Anup Karlsson. They regularly run spiritual retreats in Thailand called 'The Gathering'. Such retreats and time out, alone or with groups, are invaluable for your spiritual journey and I would highly recommend that you put some time in your diary for this work.

MEDITATION AND CONTEMPLATION

Allow yourself some time every day for meditation and contemplation. You don't need to spend a long time doing this, but do make room for a few minutes of peace. Sit comfortably with your legs uncrossed and your hands open on your knees; this will enable the energies of spirit to come to you and move through you easily. Focus on what is troubling you most at the present time, whether it be your own insecurity or your attitude to others. If you have any pain, let the pain lead you to why it's there – this will give you clues about what you need to heal.

For example, I have suffered stiff shoulders and neck for many years. Through meditation I have realised that I need to be less controlling in my work and let the responsibility of what I do rest on God's shoulders, not mine. Many of us hold responsibilities on our shoulders. They can become a burden that weighs us down and can be extremely painful too. Now I visualise myself handing over the reins of my life and work to the etheric hands of God/Spirit, and during my meditation I see myself undoing the thousands of knots that form the tight energy of my upper back. It's amazing how successful this exercise has been. At a spiritual level it has allowed me to release the burden of responsibility of my work and physically it has eased the tension and tightness that I felt before. So I recommend that you take time every day, at least for a few minutes, to look inside using a short meditation such as the one below.

Exercise to find the inner cause of your problems

In this quest to know yourself you need to understand why you have certain problems, whether these be of a physical or emotional nature. Once you understand why you have a certain problem, you can then use the many healing processes we have already covered to clear away the root cause. This meditation and visualisation will help you find the aspect of yourself that is causing any problem.

❖ Find a quiet spot which you use regularly for your inner work.

❖ Burn your favourite incense or aromatherapy oils, or spray the room with an essence that works for you. The fragrance of your incense or oils will help you trigger the intention of closing out the outside world and assist you to focus on your own energies. For example, Ripple Energy Therapy anointing oil Divine Connection holds the intention of spiritual connection and will help you keep focused in your meditation.

❖ Sit quietly, legs uncrossed and hands open to receive.

❖ Visualise yourself surrounded by a violet flame that protects you and seals your aura.

❖ Breathe in deeply four times, counting two beats at the top of each out and in breath. This slows your heartbeat and calms you mentally, emotionally and physically.

❖ Let your mind go and focus on any physical or emotional pain or mental dilemma you are wrestling with at this time.

❖ Ask the pain or concern to show you its underlying cause. Is it a fear, an old memory or an unfulfilled desire that is creating the problem? Is it self-rejection or self-doubt? Keep asking until you get some clue.

❖ Speak to your problem. Tell it you are healing it, with your own unconditional love and with the love from Spirit/God/ universal energies. Ask Spirit and God to assist you in releasing and healing the problem.

✧ Thank yourself for the fuller understanding of why you have created this situation.

✧ See divine love in the form of pink light moving to the problem area and ask your body to accept the love and healing.

✧ Thank your body for receiving the love and letting go the pain.

If you do this exercise daily you will start to understand your own involvement in the situations you are facing; you will understand yourself and the way your mind and emotions work. This is invaluable in your quest to heal and release all that comes between you and your Higher Self, and will give you a more comprehensive understanding of what makes you tick.

TOTAL ACCEPTANCE OF YOUR DIVINITY – YOUR SPIRITUAL POWER

Throughout this book I have been leading you through the understanding of your Higher Self and the healing of the barriers that come between you and your divinity. Having now seen who you are and acknowledged your personal traits, attitudes and aspects, the next step is to truly claim and connect to your divinity through acceptance. I'm talking here about your mind's capacity for acceptance – its ability to take the understanding that we have been working with and incorporate it into your belief system. I shall now share some exercises that will help you to overcome any doubts that you may still hold.

Meeting your own divine presence

The following series of meditation exercises will help you to accept and believe. You may find that you need to do them more than once. Please, don't be disheartened if you find you are not getting the response you want. I would also suggest that you find a friend or two who can share this experience with you, as this will help you hold the energy as you meditate together.

For these exercises you will need a paper or journal and pen, quiet and peaceful surroundings and the intention to be open to whatever comes into your mind or inner-sight. Trust what you receive, whether it be colours, feelings, pictures or messages. Take your time to answer the questions and don't forget also to trust your answers.

Step One

✧ Hold your pen and paper and write whatever comes to mind. Keep your eyes open or close them as it suits you, but bear in mind that most of your inner work is better done with eyes closed.

✧ Breathe in deeply four times. Breathe deep into your stomach and allow yourself time to release. Drop your shoulders and let your body relax.

✧ Visualise yourself in a beautiful garden. You are surrounded by your favourite flowers. You are safe and serene.

✧ You see coming towards you a beautiful being. This is the spiritual aspect of yourself — your divine presence.

✧ How does it feel? What do you sense? Who is it? What does it want to say?

✧ When you have all the answers or you feel the time is right, then come back to the room.

Your response

If you have received any response – whether it be a feeling, a message, a visual impression or an understanding – then you have made your connection. Well done! Both your heart and your mind have now accepted. The following exercises will help to stabilise and anchor this belief. Go to Step Two for positive response on page 219.

If you felt, sensed or saw nothing at all – not even a smidgeon – then this is because you still have unhealed wounds that are acting as barriers; your wounds are so deep that it is difficult for you to trust yourself or spirit.

Step Two – for no response

It is your mind that is stopping you accepting, so ask your mind to co-operate. Go back to Chapter 3 and repeat the integration ceremony. Then repeat Step One. If you feel or sense anything, then you can move to Step Two for a positive response. If not, then do the following exercise:

✧ Ask your mind to co-operate and be open to the possibility that you are more than a physical being.

✧ Ask yourself what lack of value within yourself inhibits you from connecting to your divine.

✧ Now write down the answers to these questions:

✧ What are you going to do now that you haven't made the connection?

✧ What can you do to release the blocks and inhibitors?

✧ What needs to occur in order for you to accept that the connection has been made?

✧ What expectations are you holding in regard to the connection? What are you expecting to feel like? What expectation of how it would seem has not been met? What was it that left you believing that the connec tion and integration did not occur?

Step Three – for no response
Ponder on what ways the connection can be made. Go beyond your expectations and think of what would let you accept the connection.

I suggest you now continue to work with the healing sessions in this book, particularly those relevant to your own needs. Spend time working with the issues that you believe are blocking you. When you are ready and feel there has been some shift in your consciousness, go through Step One again. Be gentle on yourself throughout this process and remember that you are doing nothing wrong. You haven't missed the point, but you have suffered in the past. Your understanding of yourself, your intention to heal and the work you do by following the exercises that I have shown you in this book will gradually open the doorways and release the barriers; all your wounds will slowly but surely be healed. Repeat the integration cere-mony and Step One as many times as is necessary until you have a response. Then you can move on to Step Two below.

Step Two – for positive response

Congratulations. The next step is about using the power and love that you can now access, and which are a conscious part of who you are. Again you are bringing your mind into play here, so take pen and paper and contemplate these questions for a while. Then write down your answers.

✧ What are you going to do with this power?
✧ What is your intention for the love within you?
✧ What is your next step – what are you going to do next?
✧ What are you going to do to ensure you stay connected?

There are no right or wrong answers here – just choices.

Step Three – for positive response

Ask yourself this question:

✧ What spiritual discipline would help you integrate your spirit and personality equally, so that you are not judged by yourself or others?

To give you a clue here, remember that ego can be a hurdle and can create elephant traps in our path. Any process that brings your ego back into line will be a help. Again there is no right answer, simply one that is appropriate for you. I have given you many ideas for ways to keep in balance. Find out which of them suits you – there may even be one that I have not mentioned.

Step Four – making it real

For this exercise you will need to find someone who has also made the connection, or gone through the process. This exercise is designed to make the connection truly real for you and to use the power of your own divine love to help your friend. One of you should be the giver and one the receiver.

✧ Both of you stand. Let the giver place their left hand on the heart centre (in the middle of the chest) of the receiver.

✧ Breathe and feel the energy flowing between you, creating a conduit from one to the other. Can you feel or sense the energy flowing? If not, the mind is taking control, for the energy is flowing. You are merely thinking 'I don't feel energy', or other dismissive thoughts.

✧ Swap roles now and repeat the first two steps.

✧ Now the giver – call in the light through your crown energy centre at the top of your head. Bring the energy down your left hand to the receiver's heart centre.

✧ Receiver, allow the energy into your heart and take it down through your solar plexus and through the rest of your body into the earth. Your energies are now linked.

✧ After a few minutes swap roles again. Repeat steps four and five.

✧ Now both of you sit facing each other. Both close your eyes.

✧ Giver, use your inner vision/your senses to sense and scan the receiver's energy field. Ask yourself what you can do to facilitate this person's journey. What healing do they need?

✧ Do now whatever you feel right, e.g. sweeping, energising, visualising, etc.

✧ After you have completed this process and feel that you have done enough, share your experience with your partner.

✧ Now swap roles and repeat the previous four steps.

Well done.

You now have access to your full power.

ACTIVATING THE POWERS

Now that you have not only integrated to your higher powers but also believe and accept them, I am redundant! You are on your own now . . . However, before I leave you to use your powers in whatever way you have chosen, I thought it might be a good idea to revisit them and give you a brief overview of some of the capabilities to which you have full access, and some ideas of how you can bring them into your daily life.

THE POWER OF LOVE

You will have the ability to radiate and attract love without pain, without vulnerability and without attachment. Love is the greatest healer. With love we can heal, inspire and empower ourselves and others. Start to show your love positively, both to yourself and others. Take up pastimes and learn new skills, show your self-love by positive actions and care of your body. You will be attracting love, so keep all your doors and windows open and take up any offers that appeal!

You will be attracting situations and people with the energy of love – enjoy the reactions you will now get in social and work situations. Watch the reactions to your smiles! Radiating love to everyone and everything you do will have become a natural way of being. You can use the energy of love to heal. You have done it for yourself, now you can do it for others. If you have the time, join a healing group, a support group, a hospice, a charity or a distance healing association like

Hearts and Hands (details at the back of the book). Enjoy seeing others grow, develop and flourish with your love.

THE POWER OF WISDOM

You will be in touch with the knowledge and understanding that you have accrued through many lifetimes. This is wisdom that you do not hold consciously but is part of your higher aspect. It will guide you to make good choices, and to understand yourself and the actions of others more deeply. If you allow yourself some time each day for contemplation or meditation you will be opening a channel between your higher wisdom and your mind, leaving a clear passageway for ideas and inspirations to come flowing through. If you are planning a new venture, take time out for a quiet walk, preferably in nature, to allow your Higher Self to guide you. Never underestimate the value of thinking time — sometimes this is more valuable than action. Through your connection, your own guidance will help you to make decisions based on wisdom rather than from fear.

THE POWER OF CREATION

Once you are connected, manifestation will be a given. Your thoughts will be instantly turned into reality. Remember this, for it will work with negative thoughts and visualisations just as quickly and effectively as with positive ones! So watch yourself and keep your thoughts positive at all times. You will hardly have to work at it, but to help you attract and draw towards you anything that you want, here are five steps that you can follow to transform thought into matter:

Thought to matter in five steps

✧ Hold the intention of your choice. What is it you want to attract, achieve or create?

✧ Visualise yourself receiving, being, achieving your dream. Focus on your heart centre as you do this, for example by holding your hand on your heart.

✧ Set the action in motion. Gain expertise, draw up a business or action plan, make some social engagements – whatever you need to do to make your dream a reality.

✧ Clear the barriers. If you experience any fears about your plan, check to see whether they arise from valid caution or deeper fear. If they arise from fear, work on what is causing the fear and heal the wounds behind it. Engage your will and determination – don't be put off by testing and challenging obstacles.

✧ Surrender the outcome to God. Let go the controls and let divine timing and action determine the way in which your dream will be met. Let go and let God. Go with the flow.

This process will work for both small and large dreams and needs. Don't let the size of your dream become an issue.

THE POWER OF PURPOSE

You will be in touch with the blueprint of your divine plan – the contract you made with God as to the main purpose for all your lifetimes on Earth. You also make a plan for each individual lifetime that allows you to expand on or take remedial action for what has gone before, for example opportunities to heal past wounds, to give back to those who have helped you in past lives, to take challenges to test your strengths and opportunities to grow spiritually and emotionally.

Through your integration and connection you will be linked to the energy of your purpose and blueprint. This means that you will be inspired to follow your divine path, the path you can travel with least struggle. Opportunities will abound and you will naturally draw towards you the people and situations you need to fulfil your plan. You will have a stronger sense of purpose and find it easier to make life decisions. Of course, all the decisions are yours as you utilise the power of your free will.

Another benefit of being connected is that you reclaim your free will, which is your divine right. When you are disconnected there is a strong chance that you may have let go this gift, and will feel that you are driven by the needs and desires of other people and the vagaries of life. Once you are connected, all feelings of duty and the must-dos that may have driven you before will dissolve. A strength of determination and a sense of destiny will flow through your work, your home life and every path you choose to follow.

THE POWER OF SPIRIT

When you connect to your own spiritual and divine aspect, you open the door to living and working with the Divine – with spirit. In fact, I would recommend that you ask the highly evolved beings of spirit to help you in everything you do. I never conduct a healing session or seminar without their assistance. This practice is also a good way to keep your ego under wraps! Your personal powers may be strong, but when you connect to spirit you connect to the power of the universe – to infinite love and infinite power.

As you are connected to the wisdom of all your life-times you will become more intuitive in your decision making. You will find that your psychic powers are enhanced and you will be in tune both with spirit and with your spirit guides and guardian angels. Your ability to heal and channel the energies of love will improve now that you are in tune with the immense and unconditional power of divine love. You will be opened to the powers of clairvoy-ance, clairaudience and telepathy and may start to see auras and spirit beings.

THE MAGIC OF DIVINE CONNECTION

Once connected to your own divinity it becomes natural to connect to God and the full energy of Source. Through this you have access to the power of the universe, for we are all connected by the divine source energy that flows from one to another. When you are fully connected to the heart of God all is possible. Once you are fully healed and perma-nently connected, there is no need to return to the earthly planes at the end of this lifetime. But while you are here, if you choose to be here, you can expect to create miracles on a daily basis!

Once you become fully in touch with your true self, once you are in tune with your Higher Self, once you connect to the spiritual powers, your life will change. It cannot fail to change, for you will be walking, talking and living the life of a spiritual being on Earth, and that is the most magical state of being. In this state and with this connection you will find true happiness.

Thank you for taking this journey with me.

Love and blessings

Anne

Remember who you are - spirit, divine, love, a creator, a wise being and the key to the power of the universe!

RESOURCES

WEBSITES

....

www.bwy.org.uk
The British Wheel of Yoga, governing body for yoga in Britain

www.eft-academy.co.uk
Emotional Freedom Techniques training academy

www.eftuk.org
EFT therapy for traumas, abuse, fears, phobias, depression, addiction, children's issues

www.energytherapy-direct.co.uk/EFT.html
EFT Emotional Freedom Techniques Therapy UK, list of therapists

www.nlpconnections.com
NLP Connections list of members, news, training, etc.

www.Pilates.co.uk
Pilates reference source

www.pilates-institute.com
Pilates Institute – international centres

www.sivananda.org
Official site of the International Sivananda Yoga Centres

www.taichiunion.com
Website of the Tai Chi Union for Great Britain

THERAPISTS

The following are some therapists I can recommend personally:

Hilary Hampel. Registered homeopath. Homeopathy can be used for healing the deep imprints of the past.
www.homeopathliverpool.co.uk
Email: hilaryhampel@blueyonder.co.uk
Tel: 0151 931 4116

Dee Parnell. Astrologer. A good chart can help you understand who you are, what character and personality traits you chose to bring to assist you with this life's path. Your strengths and weaknesses, opportunities and possibilities that will open up to you and when the major challenges you will face are all determined by the chart you chose before you arrived in this lifetime. She will need your date, time and place of birth and she will post you your chart.
Tel: 0779 148 4501

Janet Thompson. Past life regression therapist. A regression therapist can take you back to the hidden memories of your past, uncovering the root cause of your current problems and difficulties.
Email: mailme@janetthompson.org

Annie Lawler. Coach, counsellor and stress relief therapist. You can contact Annie at her company Breathing Space Therapies Ltd.

Website: www.breathingspacetherapies.co.uk
Email: annie@breathingspacetherapies.co.uk
Tel: 0772 581 8884

Kim White. Shaman and space clearer. Will clear the negative energies from buildings, homes and businesses. Kim travels
the world releasing the negativity that comes from invading
spirits, negative charges held in buildings and the effects of
residents' thoughts and fears.
Website:www.kimwhite.org
Email: kimwhite@ozmail.com.au

David Stevens. Chiropractor, healer and the originator of
Chiro Kinetic Therapy. A CKT therapist can talk to your
body and discover the root cause of the problem, and with
simple remedial actions can release all manner of physical,
emotional and mental problems. CKT has shown great success
for a number of problems but is particularly successful in
treating allergies.
Website: www.vitalbodyclinic.co.uk
Tel: 01372 370043

Debbie Atkinson. Healer, CKT practitioner and teacher
of 10 Step Healing using channelled natural healing energies and essential oils. For information on workshops and
sessions contact vitalbody.dorset@virgin.net

John of God. Full trance medium and healer at the spiritual and healing centre, Casa de Dom Inacio de Loyala,
Abadiania, nr Brasilia, Brazil. Phyllis Bennett is an excellent
certified guide from England I can personally recommend.
A wonderful woman who is a powerful psychic and medium
as well, she will take you through the procedures, book hotels
and guide you through your entire visit.

Website: www.healingbrazil.com
Email: healingbrazil@hotmail.com
Tel: 01375 845977

John the Beloved. A spiritually evolved master who channels advice and guidance through Helen Barton in Australia. Helen will arrange a channelled telephone session with John.
Website: www.johnthebeloved.com
Email: info@johnthebeloved.com or
johnthebeloved@bigpond.com

Claire Montanaro. A powerful channel of spiritual masters for love and guidance.
Website: www.inluminoglobal.com
Email: Claire@inluminoglobal.com
Tel: 01597 811110

Spiritual Retreat – The Gathering. Spiritual retreats in Thailand with Sandra Gonzalez and Anup Karlsson.
Website: www.lifetc.com

Brandon Bey's The Journey. Spiritual healing seminars.
Website: www.the journey.com

RECOMMENDED READING

Esther and Jerry Hicks, *The Amazing Power of Deliberate Intent: Living the Art of Allowing*, Hay House, 2006
The teachings of Abraham. Channelled messages teaching the way the Law of Attraction can work for you to allow you to manifest all you need and desire.

Anne Jones, *Heal Yourself: Simple Steps to Heal Your Emotions, Mind and Soul*, Piatkus, 2002.

Anne Jones, *Healing Negative Energies: Simple Steps to Improve Your Energy at Home and at Work*, Piatkus, 2006.

Anne Jones, *Opening Your Heart: How to Attract More Love into Your Life*, Piatkus, 2007.

Anne Jones, *The Ripple Effect*, Piatkus, 2003.

Melody, *Love is in the Earth*, Earth-love Publishing House, 1995. A book on crystals and how they can heal.

Shakuntala Modi, M.D., *Memories of God and Creation: Remembering from the Subconscious Mind*, Hampton Roads Publishing Company, 2000.

Sue Stone, *Love Life Live Life*.
Sue shares her own experiences of how to turn your life around with the power of positive thought. Order from www.suestone.com

John P. Strelecky, *The Why Are You Here Cafe: A New Way of Finding Meaning in your Life and Work*, Piatkus, 2003.

Eckhart Tolle, *The Power of Now*, Hodder Headline, 2001.

HEARTS AND HANDS FOR AFRICA

Our vision is to empower and aid those who have lost

*the ability to make choices about their wellbeing and
how they feel - those whose only choice is to face the
challenge of surviving.*

I founded Hearts and Hands for Africa to help children in
need, orphans and their carers. We have worked with Noah's
Ark, a local inner-city charity for disadvantaged women and
children, and are now focusing on Aids orphans and their
grannies in rural Zambia. Our work is supported by contri-
butions from my healing sessions, seminars and sales of my
books and CDs and from donations.

NOAH'S ARK
A shelter for children in Johannesburg, South Africa
I have long held a dream to help the babies in Africa who
have been left orphaned by Aids. The first project to fulfil this
dream was to connect to Noah's Ark in central Johannesburg,
South Africa, and buy a house. This house has become the
home for orphans and a skill centre for women who are disadvantaged or victims of Aids.

OUR PROJECT IN ZAMBIA
In Hong Kong I was extremely fortunate to befriend the
amazing Dr Cary Rosof, a medical doctor who has spent
his life working with NGOs such as Médecins Sans Frontières
to help the sick and needy in Africa.

We are creating a community farm in Mansa, Zambia, to
house and support Aids orphans and their carers, the grand-
mothers. The farm will also be a centre to teach new farming
methods that will enable the local villages to grow crops
better suited to their impoverished land.

Dr Cary's vision for our community farm project:

We are ultimately creating a blueprint for a village within a village. It will be a template that will be sound and strong and go to other places in the world as it is needed to bring people together, to promote the union of one people for the people. It will include the best technologies for global health, rejuvenating the land and supporting all its children. This model will include the best of the best and people will learn from it and adopt what they want and profit from its integrity and wisdom.

UK Charity Registration No. 1122515
21 Honey Lane, Burley, Ringwood, Hants, BH24 4EN, UK

For further information about our work please visit www.heartsandhandsforafrica.com.

ANNE JONES COLLECTION

SEMINARS AND WORKSHOPS

I run seminars and workshops covering a wide variety of topics, including:

Healers' Training Programme
Healing Events
Ten Step Healing Workshops
Healing Heart and Soul Workshops
Divine Feminine Workshops

CDS – MEDITATIONS AND VISUALISATIONS

I have recorded the meditations and exercises from my books on to a series of CDs. For further information or purchase please visit my website or contact Brenda.

BOOKS

Heal Yourself
The Ripple Effect
Opening Your Heart
The Soul Connection

CDS

Healing Visualisations 1
The Ripple Effect meditations
Opening Your Heart
The Soul Connection

JEWELLERY

I have created a range of silver jewellery using the healing symbols I use in my work. Visit my website or contact Brenda for a brochure.

HEALING

I am also available for telephone healing and have a team of healers who are available for one-to-one healing session.

Email Brenda (Brenda@annejones.org) or call 0771 075 3498 for more information.

Profits from my work and products goes to Hearts and Hands for Africa.

www.annejones.org

HEARTS AND HANDS FOR HEALING

Hearts and Hands is a non-profit-making organisation that is dedicated to spreading the use and understanding of natural energy healing.

We offer:

✧ workshops

✧ healing sessions

✧ spiritual counselling service with qualified counsellors

✧ a distance healing service

If you would like to use one of these services or become a healer on our register please visit our website: www.heartshands.org

RIPPLE ENERGY THERAPY

To assist in spreading the energies of love and healing I have created Ripple, a small company based in the peace and tranquillity of the New Forest in the west of England where we hand bottle organic essential oil blends for energy and emotional healing. Our range includes Anointing oils, Heart Balm and Aromamist sprays for clearing personal auras and rooms.

Here are a few of the blends that will be particularly helpful on your journey to your personal power:

✧ Divine Connection anointing oil – connect to the Divine and your Divine Presence

✧ Love anointing oil – receive and give love

✧ Heart Balm – heal heartache and heartbreak and attract love

✧ Letting Go anointing oil – let go the past and attachments that pull you down

✧ Manifest anointing oil – create your dreams

✧ Cleansing and Clearing AromaMist – clear negative energies around you

✧ Joy AromaMist – lift up the energies of your home and workplace

For information visit our website or contact us on info@make-ripples.com 01425 303228 or write to Ripple UK Ltd. 21 Honey Lane, Burley, Hants, BH24 4EN, UK.

All these products are available on our website: www.make-ripples.com

Profits from Ripple go to our charity Hearts and Hands for Africa.

INDEX

Note: page numbers in **bold** refer to diagrams.